UNSOLVED MYSTERIES

The Shipwreck
THOMAS HUME

Kathie,
this shipwreck
spoke to us again I
hope it speaks to
you as well.

Vaew umHerb

UNSOLVED
MYSTERIES

The Shipwreck
THOMAS HUME

The Anatomy of an Archaeological Investigation

VALERIE VAN HEEST
WILLIAM LAFFERTY

Artwork
Cover: Photograph of the bow of the *Thomas Hume* by Robert Underhill.
Back: The *Thomas Hume* as it looks on the
bottom of Lake Michigan by Robert Doornbos.
Title Graphic: Jan Underhill, J. R. Underhill Communications.

Photographs
As credited and used with permission

Published in the United States of America by In-Depth Editions, 2011
Printed in Michigan
15 14 13 12 11 10 6 5 4 3 2 1

Publisher Cataloging-in-Publication Data
van Heest, Valerie, and William Lafferty
Unsolved Mysteries: The Shipwreck *Thomas Hume* /
Valerie van Heest, William Lafferty
128 p. 80; ill., maps. cm. (Great Lakes books)
Includes bibliographical references and index (123-125)
ISBN 978-09801750-8-9 (softcover: alk paper)

1. *Thomas Hume* (schooner). 2. Shipwrecks—Great Lakes—Michigan, Lake.
3. Michigan—History. 2. Illinois—History. 3. Shipping—Michigan, Lake.
4. Shipwrecks—Michigan, Lake—History 5. Schooner Disaster—Great Lakes—
History—19th Century I. Title II. Author

2011
910.453   2011905452
Soft Cover Edition

"Wooden ships and iron men succumb to the mighty seas and the God that made them, leaving their unfinished journeys and lives without record, possibly waiting for the wreck diver to finally report their stories and bring them at last home to port."

an excerpt from "The Marked Man,"
a poem by Bud Brain.

This book is dedicated to Bud Brain, an explorer with curiosity, talent, and enthusiasm. He is an inspiration.

UNSOLVED MYSTERIES

Table of
CONTENTS

Valerie van Heest gears up for a deep dive. Photograph by Jack van Heest.

FOREWORD

And
AUTHOR NOTES

I heard about an amazingly intact shipwreck in the fall of 2007. Chicago-based diver Jeff Strunka, a man I had known when I served as director of the Underwater Archaeological Society of Chicago (UASC), described the three-masted schooner recently found by Chicago marine salvors A & T Recovery in all its glory—upright, intact, and loaded with artifacts. He indicated that he and his associates, Tom Palmisano, Bud Brain, and Bob Schmitt, believed it to be the long-missing schooner *Thomas Hume*, a tidbit that only served to increase my interest.

I had researched the *Hume*, a lumber schooner lost in mysterious circumstances while owned by its namesake Thomas Hume, a Muskegon, Michigan, lumber baron, whose home on Webster Avenue in Muskegon, Michigan, is now an historic site owned and operated by the Lakeshore Museum Center. Although Jeff had not disclosed the location of the shipwreck, he indicated it was in deep water far off the shores of Chicago; I presumed within Illinois waters. However, its strong connection to Michigan's rich lumbering history interested me. While I enjoy diving shipwrecks—the more intact the better—I am interested in the information contained in these time capsules that can add to the collective base of maritime knowledge. Over the last twenty years, I have co-founded three non-profit organizations, the missions of which are to interpret maritime history: The UASC, the Southwest Michigan Underwater Preserve, and most recently Michigan Shipwreck Research Associates (MSRA). During that time, I have written several books, archaeological reports, popular articles, and documentary scripts about the shipwrecks we have studied. I asked Jeff if he might consider allowing MSRA to become involved in surveying the *Thomas Hume*.

Although Jeff considered my request, he considered a survey premature. He and his dive partners had yet to find positive proof—in the way of a name board or hull numbers—of the vessel's identity. Complicating their efforts, they had not been able to find a photograph of the *Hume* and only had measurements and a basic description to compare to lists of ships gone missing. Jeff indicated their team planned to spend the summer diving the wreck, and if they could prove the vessel was the *Hume*, he would contact me.

I took it upon myself to search through known maritime archives for an image of the *Thomas Hume* and soon made a discovery: a photograph labeled *H. C. Albrecht*, the schooner that would be later renamed *Thomas Hume*. However, the image created more problems than it solved. The divers indicated that there were features on the wreck that did not match the schooner in the photograph. Discouraged, we all went back to the drawing board. Although I thoroughly searched a number of shipwreck databases and archives, I could not turn up any other possibilities of three-masted schooners gone missing in Lake Michigan that resembled the schooner on the bottom. That's when I began to question the provenance of the photograph. If the wreck *was* the *Thomas Hume,* then perhaps the schooner in the photograph was not. I made a trip to the archive to examine the glass plate from which the photograph had been made to see if I could read the name board. I discovered that the photograph had been mislabeled. It was, in fact, an image of the *Home,* not the *Hume.* Although we still did not have a photograph of the *H.C.Albrecht/Thomas Hume,* the possibility remained that the wreck was in fact the *Thomas Hume.*

Other MSRA projects directed my attention away from this wreck, but its mystery continued to intrigue me. In the fall of 2008, the Association for Great Lakes Maritime History invited me to speak at its annual conference scheduled that year in Muskegon. Although I planned to present information about a variety of West Michigan shipwrecks, the conference's location in the former home port of the *Thomas Hume* compelled me to ask Jeff Strunka if I might share a bit of his underwater video with the conference participants. By then, he and his teammates had explored the wreck from bow to stern and although they had not found any positive markings to identify it as the *Thomas Hume,* they had found nothing to disprove it. Jeff gave me his approval.

The underwater images of the wreck ignited quite an interest among those who attended. Elizabeth Sherman, great granddaughter of Thomas Hume and a maritime author who presented the story of the *Thomas Hume* at the same conference, was thrilled to learn that the mystery of its disappearance might finally be solved. At the conference, I met Dani LaFleur, an underwater archaeologist and collections manager at the Lake Shore Museum Center in Muskegon. Although her day-to-day work at the museum did not involve underwater archaeology, she became very interested in the wreck. A reporter for Muskegon's local paper saw the program and wrote a story about the *Thomas Hume's* discovery. Folksinger and songwriter Lee Murdock also attended the presentation. The underwater footage apparently inspired him. He called me several weeks later and asked if he could sing a song over the phone. It's not every day that a famous maritime crooner calls me to sing, so I gathered the family around the phone, put it on speaker mode, and listened to his beautiful a capella tune and haunting title, "I'm Still Here." His song made me feel as if the schooner had spoken to me.

Later that year, I received the phone call for which I had been waiting. Tom Palmisano, Jeff's partner, asked if I was still interested in becoming involved in a survey of the vessel believed to be the *Thomas Hume.* He gave me the coordinates for the wreck and within a few weeks, the MSRA team dived the site. What we saw made us realize this shipwreck was worthy of not only a survey, but also full archaeological study and potentially a museum exhibit and documentary film. In short order, we formed a partnership with the Lake Shore Museum Center. To our good fortune, in addition to Dani LaFleur, John McGarry, the museum's executive director, is also experienced in underwater archaeology and fully supported the project. Lee Murdock soon joined the team, offering to score original music for the documentary. Then, William Lafferty, with whom I had written a previous book, offered his research talents. MSRA's board members, Jack van Heest and Craig Rich, and MSRA's dive team, Robert and Jan Underhill, Jeff Vos, Todd White, and Tim Marr, all offered to lend their skills documenting the wreck. Artist Bob Doornbos threw his ink pens and paintbrush into the mix as well, and Kendall College students Melissa Anys and Jennifer Gustafson offered their computer animation skills. To make all this possible, I applied for and received a grant from the Michigan Humanities Council to underwrite significant portions of the project. Subsequently, the Great Lakes Shipwreck Research Foundation, the Great Lakes Cruising Club, and the Gertz Foundation offered additional grants. Along the way archaeologists David Copper, Ken Pott, John McManamon, Keith Merviden, and Tamara Thompson, and historians C. Patrick Labadie, Joel Stone, and Thom Holden offered information and input. Although a book was not part of the original plans, the archaeological evidence discovered on the wreck during the summer of 2010 seemed too significant to go unpublished.

I wish to extend my appreciation to all of the individuals and organizations mentioned. John McGarry and Dani LaFleur's archaeological expertise proved invaluable, and the staff at the Lakeshore Museum Center, including Mindy Conley, Joni Dorsett, Beryl Gabel, Lorene Vandermeer, and Melissa Horton, provided valuable input and assistance. I am especially thankful to my business partner Bill Lafferty who researched the career of the *H. C. Albrecht/Thomas Hume*; wrote, in large part, chapter four; and consulted with me on the balance of the book. His attention to detail and ability to locate previously undiscovered historical information is a gift. Many thanks to author Neel Zoss and historian Ed Warner of the Association for Great Lakes Maritime History for reading and commenting on the manuscript. And, as always, I am thankful to Ann Weller for her proofreading.

In the end, our team solved the mystery of the *Hume*'s disappearance, but the collection of shoes, clothing, jewelry, coins, and tools found inside it generated even more mysteries. What fun would life be without a good mystery?

Valerie van Heest

This may have been how the Thomas Hume *looked sailing out of Chicago into building seas on May 21, 1891. Graphic by Valerie van Heest.*

CHAPTER ONE

A Mysterious DISAPPEARANCE

The career of the schooner *Thomas Hume* ended on May 21, 1891, under mysterious circumstances that baffled even the most experienced lake men at the time. Under the command of Captain Harry Albrightson with First Mate Olaf Johnson and with a crew of five other men, the vessel headed out of Chicago running light in the company of the *Rouse Simmons* (a schooner that would later gain fame as the Christmas Tree ship) on a return trip to Muskegon. The weather turned bad during the run, prompting the captain of the *Simmons* to return to Chicago to wait out the blow. The *Thomas Hume* continued on, never to be seen again. Thomas Hume, namesake of the vessel, and Charles Hackley, the Muskegon, Michigan-based lumber barons who shared in ownership of the schooner, were shocked that their staunchly built vessel could go missing. In fact, they reported nothing amiss for almost one week, expecting that the vessel would show up in one of Lake Michigan's many ports. But when it did not, they abandoned all hope and shared their worst fears with the local newspaper. The *Muskegon Chronicle* on May 28, 1891, reported the story of the disappearance:

"The schooner Thomas Hume, owned by Hackley & Hume, of this city, has undoubtedly been wrecked and gone to the bottom of Lake Michigan, together with her crew of seven men. Last Thursday evening one week ago, the Hume and the Rouse Simmons left Chicago to come to Muskegon. A pretty stiff gale was blowing at the time and although lake Michigan was somewhat rough, the officers of the boats thought they could make the trip safely. Most of the lumber barges, however, did not look at it in the same light and quietly remained in Chicago until the next day.

The Hume and Simmons skipped along pretty lively and encountered a heavy sea. The Simmons labored in the storm several hours and put back into Chicago, arriving there that night again. The last seen of the Hume she was encountering the storm and pursuing her course to Muskegon.

The Simmons remained in Chicago until the storm subsided and then made her way to Muskegon. Upon arriving here the captain was much surprised to learn that the Hume had not shown up. At first, it was expected that she had drifted out of her course and run in somewhere for shelter, but days passed and no tidings being received of her whereabouts, naturally, fears arose as to her safety. Enquiries were made of officers of the other boats, but none had heard or seen of the Hume nor detected any wreckage which might denote that she had been wrecked.

Efforts to find any traces of the boat were unavailing, so this morning her owners Messrs, Hackley & Hume abandoned all hope. The schooner Thomas Hume was formerly the H. C. Albright, and is familiar to all mariners. In Chicago last winter she was thoroughly rebuilt and rated A2. She was in charge of Capt. Harry Albrightson, whose home is in Chicago. Besides the captain, she had a crew of six men, but at this time, it is not known where their families or relatives reside. The Hume was valued at $6,500."[1]

At the same time as the articles ran in newspapers throughout the Great Lakes region and beyond, Thomas Hume informed his wife of the disaster that befell his namesake vessel in a letter he mailed to her in Belfast, Ireland, where she and their daughters were vacationing at the time. In his own hand he wrote:

"We have had a marine disaster here, which has put rather a damper on us. The Hume left Chicago last Thursday evg (8 days ago) for Muskegon in the company with the Simmons. They separated out in Lake Michigan, they had head wind, and on Friday, the Simmons ran back to Chicago. The Hume did not run back, but stayed outside. The Simmons left Chicago again on Saturday and got here Monday morning. We looked for the Hume here same time, but it did not come Monday, nor Tuesday, nor Wednesday and has not come yet. If she had run into any port, we would have heard from her, and if she was afloat she ought to have been here Monday. It is now Friday, and as nothing has been heard from her so we have reluctantly concluded that this must be lost with all hands. We do not know how she could be lost except by capsizing, (which is almost impossible) or collision in which both boats may have gone to the bottom. There has not been any weather stormy enough but what she could take care of herself or anything like as bad as what she has gone through a great many times before. We don't mind the loss of the boat very much, but don't like losing the seven men on board her. Harry Albrightson was captain; you know him as the man with a deep bass voice, and he was a first-class sailor. We intend to send a tug out tonight to look for her, and can probably find her if she capsized. I was in Chicago Wednesday, but we have so far had no definite knowledge of her since she left Chicago. Harry had a wife and several children. I don't know anything about the families of the other men."[2]

The loss of his vessel and the crew was undoubtedly hard for Thomas Hume, especially in the wake of another recent disaster. The city of Muskegon was still dealing with the aftermath of the May 16, 1891, fire, known as the Pine Street fire, which destroyed 17 city blocks and 250 buildings including the original courthouse. It had been very dry that May, and the lack of rain contributed to the blaze. When the rain finally came on May 21, the people of western Michigan were certainly overjoyed, but the winds that accompanied the rain could have contributed to the loss of the *Thomas Hume*. However, newspaper

A similar size and type schooner also riding light, the Fleetwing *appears as the* Thomas Hume *may have on its last day, fighting the storm in an attempt to reach Muskegon, Michigan.*

stories that ran throughout the Midwest actually reported conflicting weather accounts. The *Buffalo Enquirer* of May 29, 1891, reported that there had been no rough weather since the *Hume* sailed from Chicago, yet the *Port Huron Daily Times* of the same date noted that when the *Hume* and the *Rouse Simmons* left Chicago, a storm raged.

Conflicting weather accounts were not the only errors reported. Anytime a ship goes missing with all crew, there exists the possibility that speculation will run wild. In the case of the *Thomas Hume,* speculation fueled by sensationalistic reporting, combined with simple mistakes, built this one vessel loss into a mystery of massive proportions. After the initial news announcement made by Hackley and Hume in Muskegon on May 28, reporters in Muskegon followed the story and newspapers throughout the Midwest picked it up as well. The May 29, 1891, *Muskegon Morning News* reported the *Thomas Hume*'s loss as "shrouded in mystery," indicating that vessel men believed that "the boat was fighting her way along the west coast in the teeth of a gale and ran into the path of one of the big iron ore freighters and went down in a collision." Newspapers in Chicago interviewed Benjamin Franklin Deming, the lumber agent for Hackley & Hume. Deming thought a collision possible but he also knew that the weather had been bad and might have sunk the *Hume*. In either case, he believed the accident occurred within twenty miles of Chicago and the vessel would have been dragged toward the head of the lake. Chicago papers interjected mystery into the story reporting that some sailors hinted that the *Hume* may not have been seaworthy. Reporters questioned Captain Dunham, a well-respected tugboat fleet owner in Chicago, who had heard reports from one of his pilots that the *Hume* had been leaking that spring. Likewise, Secretary Lindboltz of the Seaman's Union knew nothing personally of the vessel's seaworthiness, but had talked to a crewman of the *Hume*, Saxe Larson, who made two trips on the schooner that spring. Larson told him that the *Hume* had been leaking badly. In fact, Larson had been scheduled to sail on the May 21 run, but had been delayed in some way that morning and did not make it to the boat in time.[3]

Despite the whirlwind of reporting, no one knew much about the missing crew,

Thomas Hume as he looked later in life. Lakeshore Museum Center Collection.

even Hackley & Hume officials in Muskegon. Hackley and Hume reasoned that the ship's book listing the crew was lost with the vessel. Some papers reported that speculation ran high in Chicago regarding who was on board. Apparently, assumptions were proven wrong when those believed lost with the vessel eventually showed up in Chicago. However, Deming probably had been at the dock to receive the last load, and would have had some idea of who made up the crew. He later confirmed for reporters that Harry Albrightson had been captain; in fact he knew Albrightson and his wife well. He also knew Olaf Johnson had served as first mate and reported that he was a single man who left a brother and sister in Chicago and parents in the "old country," likely Sweden.[4] In addition, he reported that Peter Andrea Espon served as steward. Chris Peterson, Oscar Anderson, Charles Anderson, and one other Scandinavian were on board as sailors. All called Chicago their home.[5] However, one simple error made by one newspaper and picked up by many—the addition of an apostrophe—confused the matter of who went missing with the *Hume* for more than a century. Several papers reported that Harry Albright's son captained the schooner on its last run.

Hackley and Hume clearly accepted their schooner gone, but had difficulty believing that a storm overcame the staunchly built and newly repaired vessel, instead assuming that another vessel had rammed the *Hume*, never reporting the accident. Despite the recent sinking of the three-year-old scow schooner *W. C. Kimball* that went missing in a spring gale on Lake Michigan off Little Sable point just two weeks earlier—the first vessel loss on the Great Lakes during 1891—no one could imagine that the *Thomas Hume* shared the same fate. In fact, they had a difficult time accepting a storm as the cause for the *Kimball*'s loss. However, more than sixty vessels would follow the *Kimball* and the *Hume* to the bottom of the Great Lakes during the 1891 shipping season alone. Almost one-third of those losses took place on Lake Michigan, which has the reputation of being one of the most dangerous lakes among her four sisters. Lake men and ship owners working at the time of the *Hume*'s loss would have also been keenly familiar with the disasters of the previous season in which over seventy vessels sank or broke up throughout the Great Lakes, 25 percent of them in Lake Michigan. Of great curiosity is why Hackley & Hume could not fully accept that its schooner, although twenty-one years old, a middle-aged lake vessel at the time, could sink in a storm as so many others had. This gives reason to consider the common human notion that accidents only happen to other people.

In the weeks that followed the disappearance of the *Thomas Hume* in late May 1891, Charles Hackley and Thomas Hume hoped to find positive proof of what befell their schooner, either wreckage from the *Hume* to suggest a collision, or the capsized hull still floating on the surface. Hackley & Hume commissioned Captain Christian of the tug *Henry S. Sill* to search the route from Muskegon to Chicago and all around the head of the lake. The *Sill* left Saturday, May 30, with Captain Seth Lee aboard representing Hackley & Hume and it arrived in Chicago on June 1, having found nothing. From there, the searchers traveled to St. Joseph, Michigan, and then down to Michigan City, Indiana, where Lee telegraphed Hackley on the morning of June 2 to report they had found not the slightest trace of any wreckage at the head of the lake. The search continued as Charles Hackley spoke to reporters that same morning.

Hackley thought that whatever happened must have occurred unexpectedly because he felt otherwise the crew would have taken to the lifeboat and made it to shore. Convinced the *Hume* had been run down, he offered a $300 reward for any information about the accident, hoping that amount would "remove the seal of secrecy that some recreant captain may have set upon his crew."[6] In addition, the same article showed Hackley's disbelief that an accident could befall *his* vessel and *his* captain despite so many other vessels sinking in storms on the Great Lakes:

> "In 19 years we have been running our own vessels, this is the first serious accident. We never had a schooner go on the beach. All our vessels were kept in first class condition and the captains always had instructions to get whatever they considered necessary for the security of the crew without asking for special permission. The Hume had $2000 spent on her in repairs the last winter. She carried a first class lifeboat and everything to insure the safety of the crew in case of accident."[7]

Likewise, Lee held onto the belief that another vessel had rammed the *Hume*, and sailed away to avoid blame. The *Muskegon Chronicle* reported his thoughts:

> "Collision, run down, of course just as the *W. C. Kimball* was run down. If she capsized she wouldn't sink, and I don't believe that the staunch, stiff vessel ever capsized. Some steamer ran her down. People say no captain would be heartless enough to leave a crew after running their vessel down. Pshaw! I have sailed these lakes forty years and I know of several such cases. The fine schooner *Magellen* was one of them. If the officers see a big loss to pay for, you bet they keep mum."

Lee still expected to eventually find hatch covers, masts, portions of the deckhouse, or even the schooner's small boat floating upon the surface of the lake as evidence of such foul play, as had been the case with the *Magellan*. Fourteen years earlier on November 11, 1877, the *Magellan* foundered with the loss of eight crew off Manitowoc, Wisconsin. The *Manitowoc County Chronicle* of November 13, 1877 reported the incident:

> "On Friday morning the spars of a vessel, which proved to be the Magellan, … loaded with 20,000 bushels of corn, bound from Chicago to Toronto, were seen sticking out of the water a short distance northeast of the harbor piers… The cause of the disaster is at present unknown, and perhaps may never be known. Some are of the opinion that she sprung a leak, owing to injuries received while being towed out of the Chicago River, and that she became unmanageable in the heavy seas. Others at Manitowoc are firm in the belief that she was run down while at anchor off the point by one of the large Lake Superior propellers. The Inter-Ocean of yesterday intimates that a collision occurred between the schooners Magellan and Neelon, and that both vessels are sunk near this place."

Later speculation suggested that the *Joseph L. Hurd* was involved in the sinking of the *Magellan* because bodies found washed upon the shore after the accident showed evidence of having "been through the propeller of some boat, one having an arm cut off, another a large chunk of flesh ripped from the back."[8] However, forty-four years later the *Manitowoc Herald* of November 8, 1922, laid this to rest when it printed, "Reports current at the time that the *Magellan* had been struck and sunk by the steamer *Hurd*, which later put into port here for shelter, were never proved."

Seth Lee's cynicism about the *Magellan* must have affected his thoughts about what befell the *Thomas Hume* more than a decade later. Although he hoped to find evidence of a collision floating upon the surface of the lake, Lee returned to Muskegon in early June to report his lack of success. In fact, no other steamers or schooners traveling that busy course over the last two weeks had reported any signs of the *Thomas Hume*.[9]

Seth Lee, a well-respected captain for Hackley & Hume, assisted in the search for the missing Thomas Hume *and held onto the belief that a steamer rammed it and sailed away to avoid liability. Lakeshore Museum Center Collection.*

The mystery thickened after the *Henry S. Sill's* failed expedition. On June 9, 1891, the *Muskegon Chronicle* reported a startling rumor originating in Chicago. "There was a wild and wooley suggestion that the Hume might have gone to some obscure port, been repainted and changed her name, and been sailed to some other portion of the lake."[10] However, a well-known vessel man in Chicago, whose identity was not mentioned, countered that opinion, "The case of the Hume is one of the most mysterious we have ever had on the lake. If she had been loaded and sunk, her hatches would have been forced out and floated. If she went down light, there would have been something that would have floated and been discovered." But he did not believe the *Hume* had been stolen and renamed, "Vessels have countenances like human beings. There is something different in the build of each one, and I can stand in the window of my office and tell the name of any vessel coming up the river, even when she is a block or two away. It would be impossible for the Hume to pass by here without my recognizing her. At the same time, there is something mysterious about her disappearance."[11]

Harry Albrightson's wife had no choice but to accept her husband's loss. She had six children to care for and a home on Ayers Court in Chicago. Her husband had been employed by Hackley & Hume for twelve years.[12] Just over a month after the disappearance, she appealed to the Chicago Guarantee Life Insurance fund to pay her $2000 policy on the life of her husband without going into the courts. Normally the insurance company would require proof of death, but by that point there was no doubt that he had been lost with his ship.[13]

Just after the story of the *Hume*'s loss began to settle and Hackley & Hume got back to the business of shipping lumber, on August 13, 1891, three months after the *Hume*'s disappearance, a note in a bottle washed ashore near Benton Harbor, Michigan. Inside, handwritten words on brown paper seemed to explain the *Hume*'s disappearance:

"We the undersigned are the passengers of the Thomas Hume. The schooner's hold is rapidly filling with water and we have no hope of escape. We are on the St. Joseph course and been drifting for hours. We have friends In McCook, Neb. and Elkhart, Ind. Please notify them of our fate. Frank Maynard and Wilbur Grover."[14]

The *Omaha Daily Bee* office in Chicago never even considered the note truthful. On August 15, 1891, it offered opinion that the message in the bottle was a fraud, noting, "Vessel men look upon it as the work of a bottle fiend." The article suggested how improbable it would have been for the schooner to have carried passengers and how even more improbable it would be that men hailing from Nebraska and Indiana could determine that the vessel was on the St. Joseph course. In fact, the *Thomas Hume*'s regular route was on a course line between Chicago and Muskegon, much farther north than the St. Joseph course line. Charles Hackley also dismissed this claim, indicating that only crew would have been aboard. B. F. Deming, Hackley & Hume's business agent in Chicago, substantiated this, indicating he believed the vessel had not taken on any passengers. Deming felt the bottle's note would aggravate Mrs. Albrightson's condition since she had been prostrate with grief since her husband's death. He was glad to know that her friends went to great lengths to keep news of the bottle discovery away from her.[15]

Fourteen years would pass before someone would come forth to offer proof of the *Thomas Hume*'s sinking, but by then Hackley's $300 reward for evidence of the accident had been long forgotten. On October 9, 1905, a fisherman's nets became entangled in a shipwreck three miles off New Buffalo, Michigan, in 56 feet of water. The fisherman reported the loss of his net to Captain A. A. Kent of the Life Saving Station of Michigan City, Indiana, who, with his crew and diver George Culbert, went to New Buffalo the next day to dive to the wreck. Speculation ran high at the time that the wreck might be the steamer *Chicora* lost just ten years earlier in 1895, with 25 men. However, Culbert found instead a three-masted schooner, which the *Herald Palladium* reported to be 175 feet long, noting that Culbert thought it might be the *Thomas Hume*. Since most maritime people, including Culbert, would have been aware that the *Hume* was significantly smaller than that, it is quite possible that the paper made a mistake in reporting the length of the wreck. George Culbert indicated that he searched the wrecked schooner carefully for a name, but found none.[16] He also noted that the vessel's hold was nearly filled with sand and that it was impossible to search inside for the remains of the crew.[17] Apparently, no one considered that the shipwreck might be the 136-foot-long sailing vessel *John V. Ayer* lost in November 1856 somewhere south of St. Joseph, Michigan, a more likely candidate considering that, after more than fifty years underwater, the shifting currents in shallow water could contributed to it filling with sand. It also seems apparent that no one believed Culbert had actually dived on the *Thomas Hume* because reports continued about the missing schooner over the subsequent decades.

The Mystery Lived On

In 1937, Fred A. Ebersole, the writer of the *Chicago Tribune*'s column "In the Wake of the News," perpetuated the mystery of the *Hume* after speaking with H. L. Saunders, retired superintendent of a steamship line and a sixty-two-year veteran of the Lakes. Saunders recalled the lake was rough on the day the *Hume* and the *Simmons* left Chicago, but there was no storm. "Loss of the Hume and its crew without leaving a trace on one of the most traveled lake routes remains to this day one of the most mysterious disappearances in the history of the Great Lakes."

As the years passed, and the people who knew of the *Hume* passed as well, its legacy lived on. Several books recount the story with the same drama as H. L. Saunders did. Even a song appeared, although its origin is unknown. When researching their book, *Windjammers, Songs of the Great Lakes*, authors Ivan Walton and Joe Grimm quoted William Nicholas of the Steamboat Inspection Service office in Chicago, who recalled in 1933 a song about the *Thomas Hume* that he had learned about forty years earlier as a young man sailing the Great Lakes. Unfortunately, like so many previous accounts of the loss of the *Thomas Hume*, the song spawns more errors, including the date of the accident, the cargo, and the destination. However, unlike so many previous accounts, the songwriter accepted the notion that a storm caused the vessel to sink, the likeliest of all possibilities, yet a possibility those closest to the vessel were unable to accept.

> The schooner Hume is staunch and strong,
> She's weathered many a blow,
> Her hold is full of prairie wheat,
> She's bound for Buffalo.
>
> Lake Michigan is long and wide,
> Lake Michigan is deep,
> And gallant sailors man her ships,
> Their friends for some do weep.
>
> The old man walks the after deck,
> He eyes the evening sky;
> "All hands aboard—Cast off! Says he,
> "Cast off!" the mate replies.
>
> She tows out of the river mouth,
> Aloft her flowing sail;
> She clears Chicago's harbor light
> Before a sou'west gale.

The Hume fears no late-season storm,
All gallant lads her crew;
It's double rates and double pay,
Her canvas all is new.

The cabin boy looked long to land,
The old man out to sea;
The mate casts anxious looks aloft,
"all hands stand by," says he.

They're sailing on the northern star
Well off the western shore,
November seas break on her deck,
And long her bulworks roar.

The wind hauls north and bares its teeth,
An' mountainous grow the seas;
They wash across her slanting decks
An' on her riggin' freeze.

The night comes on all thick and dark,
She disappears from view—
And that's the last was ever seen
Of that gallant ship and crew!

November night are anxious nights
For the sailor's friends ashore—
November days are mournful days
When the vessel is seen no more![18]

More than a century after the *Hume*'s loss, modern books and web sites about strange phenomena rank the *Thomas Hume* among the more mysterious of vessel disappearances. In her book *Weird Michigan*, author Linda S. Godfrey attributes the disappearance of the *Thomas Hume* to the "Michigan Triangle" (much like the Bermuda Triangle), which she notes falls between Ludington, Michigan, Benton Harbor, Michigan, and Manitowoc, Wisconsin. A web site entitled "Phantoms and Monsters" notes, "Among the strangest of the mysteries is the disappearance of the schooner *Thomas Hume*, which disappeared without a trace in a Lake Michigan gale on May 21, 1891, while sailing empty from Chicago to Muskegon, Michigan, to pick up a load of lumber. Seven sailors, including Captain George C. Albrecht, were lost with the ship…To this day, the *Hume*'s disappearance remains unsolved." The mistake made by newspapers in 1891 in reporting the captain as Harry Albright's son (instead of Harry Albrightson), has apparently carried forth to the present. In fact, the original vessel owner H. C. Albrecht had a son, George, who became a lake master. Many immigrants with the name "Albrecht" Americanized their names to "Albright," a sheer coincidence that may have led to the perpetuation of the original error. Today web sites like the one mentioned above, and even maritime archives like that of Bowling Green State University, list George C. Albrecht as the captain who died on the *Thomas Hume*. The discovery of George C. Albrecht's census records and obituary confirm that he was indeed the son of H. C. Albrecht, the original owner and master of the *H.C. Albrecht*, but he was not in command of the *Thomas Hume* when it went missing. Instead, George Albrecht died three years after the loss of the *Hume* in 1894, soon after an attack of "the grippe," an influenza referred to today as the flu, as reported in his obituary.[19]

Although this small mystery has easily been solved, many more questions linger: Did the *Thomas Hume* go down in the storm? Did another vessel ram and sink the *Thomas Hume*? Did the crew steal the schooner and sail away? Was the note in the bottle true or a hoax? Did the *Thomas Hume* really sink in just 56 feet of water off New Buffalo, Michigan? One web site at the time of this writing posted a prophetic comment: "Until sport divers confirm that the wreck of the *Hume* lies somewhere at the bottom of Lake Michigan, there will remain a doubt in some minds that the vessel ever sank."[20]

---

1   "With all on board," *Muskegon Chronicle,* May 29, 1891.
2   Hume, Thomas, Personal Correspondence. Michigan State University Archives and Historical Collections, Hackley & Hume Papers, 1859-1955. 00097
3   "Sound as a Bell," *Muskegon Chronicle,* May 31, 1891.
4   *Buffalo Enquirer,* June 2, 1891.
5   "They call it all a hoax," *Chicago Daily Tribune.* August 15, 1891.
6   "The Missing Schooner," *Muskegon Chronicle.* June 2, 1891.
7   Ibid.
8   *Manitowoc Herald,* November 8, 1922.
9   *Muskegon Chronicle*, June 3, 1891.
10   "The Missing Schooner," *Muskegon Chronicle.* June 9, 1891.
11   Ibid.
12   "With all on board," *Muskegon Chronicle,* May 29, 1891.
13   *The Daily Interocean,* July 7, 1891.
14   "Probably a hoax," *Muskegon Chronicle.* August 14, 1891.
15   "They call it all a hoax," *Chicago Daily Tribune*, August 15, 1891.
16   *Herald Palladium,* October 10, 1905.
17   Although in 1905, many likely believed the wreck off New Buffalo was the *Hume*, Culbert overlooked another possibility. On November 4, 1856, the three-masted schooner *John V. Ayer*, a vessel virtually the same size as the *Hume*, was lost reportedly off St. Joseph, Michigan (about twenty miles north of New Buffalo). It foundered with 17,000 bushels of wheat and the loss of ten crewmen. Culver could have been mistaken in saying the vessel had filled with sand. Perhaps over the fifty years since the *Ayer's* loss, sand had covered the wheat cargo making it appear to be full. Perhaps one day divers will rediscovery the three-masted schooner off New Buffalo and confirm its identity.
18   Walton, Ivan and Joe Grimm, *Windjammers, Songs of the Great Lakes* (Detroit: Wayne State University Press, 2002), 197.
19   *Manitowoc Pilot,* January 18, 1894.
20   http://www.perdurabo10.tripod. November 2010.

Looking toward the bow of the Thomas Hume *from the lake bottom 145 feet beneath the surface of Lake Michigan. Photograph by Robert Underhill.*

CHAPTER
TWO

Discovery of a
TIME CAPSULE

The story of the *Thomas Hume*'s mysterious disappearance was the last thing on the minds of divers and commercial salvors Al Olson and Taras Lysenko of A & T Recovery as they piloted their boat *Brigantine* slowly back and forth across the water in the southern end of Lake Michigan on July 25, 1995. They stayed focused on their tasks of maintaining a straight heading, keeping an eye on the plotter, and making sure the cable and tow fish running out behind the boat did not become entangled in anything. Lysenko and Olson were conducting search operations that day, just as they had done many hundreds of days previously. Using a 100 kHz Edge Tech side-scan sonar, the men were looking for a downed military airplane presumed lost in that general vicinity during a training mission in the 1940s. The transducer on the tow fish they used emits pulses of sound shot horizontally across the lake bottom, which reflect off any objects that project above the bottom. The strength and travel time of the reflected pulses are recorded and processed into an image that prints out on the paper plotter.

Since the late 1980s, A&T Recovery has been the United States Navy's primary contractor for the recovery of World War II airplanes lost in Lake Michigan. In 1942 the Navy began qualifying pilots for aircraft carrier landings and take-offs from two former passenger liners, the *Sea and Bee* and the *Greater Buffalo*, which had been converted to aircraft carriers, becoming the USS *Wolverine* and the USS *Sable*. The Navy trained over 15,000 pilots between 1942 and 1945, during which time several aircraft were lost. Decades later, those lost planes have become historical treasures. A & T has located and recovered over thirty airplanes, most of which have been sent to the National Museum of Naval Aviation in Pensacola, Florida, for restoration and display.[1]

On that spring day, A & T watched as the plotter stylus pulsed back and force, beginning the outline of an anomaly they immediately realized was something of substantial size on the bottom at about 145 feet deep. Familiar with the kind of image that a small, single-engine plane would make, they quickly realized this anomaly was too big to be an airplane. To the untrained eye, the image appeared to be little more than a smudge, but Olson and Lysenko had interpreted dozens of such images. Based on the size and shape, they realized they had discovered a schooner and it appeared to have three masts.

In the course of its normal work, A&T Recovery has located a number of sites in lower basin of Lake Michigan other than airplanes, including the remains of a prehistoric

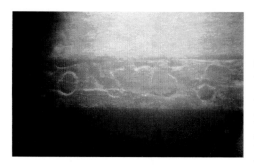

Divers with the UASC discovered the registration number of the Wells Burt *carved into the main beam. Although a marine regulation, such numbers are not often found on shipwrecks. UASC Collection.*

forest, the German World War I submarine *UC-97*, a war prize scuttled off shores of northern Illinois as a requirement of the Versailles Treaty, and several shipwrecks. As the busiest port in the Great Lakes, Chicago's high commercial traffic resulted in a proportionately high number of shipwrecks. However, with the lake bottom generally shallow at the southern end of the lake, shipwrecks tend to take a beating from the waves and action of the winter ice, leaving little but a scattering of planks and machinery.

In 1988, A & T discovered a schooner in shallow water off Evanston, Illinois, that it immediately realized was unique. The entire lower hull and deck were intact, having settled into the silt lake bottom up to its waterline. Dozens of artifacts lay scattered on the deck and in the debris field. Clearly, the vessel had never been dived upon, and to a firm keenly aware of the condition of sunken vessels it represented the most intact schooner yet found in the southern third of Lake Michigan. From manufacturer's marks on the forward capstan and hull numbers carved into the main beam (much like a vehicle identification number today), they were able to identify it as the *Wells Burt,* a three-masted schooner lost in a storm in 1883. Recognizing the wreck as an archaeological time capsule, and also recognizing the lure that a virgin wreck poses to divers intent upon pilfering artifacts as souvenirs, A & T sought the involvement of the Underwater Archaeological Society of Chicago. A new organization at the time, the UASC's mission involved the documentation and preservation of shipwrecks.

The UASC sprang up in the wake of the Abandoned Shipwreck Act enacted by Congress in 1988. This new statute turned over responsibility and management of abandoned shipwrecks, those in which the owner has relinquished rights, and which are embedded in the bottomlands or eligible for the National Register of Historic Places, to the states on whose bottomlands they rest. In turn, each of the Great Lakes states enacted regulations to maximize the enhancement of these cultural resources by fostering partnerships among the people who use them in some way like divers, fishermen, archaeologists, scientists, and salvors. The most significant new development affecting divers involved the establishment of laws that make recovering artifacts illegal without a permit. Several volunteer organizations like the UASC began cropping up around the Great Lakes in the wake of the new law to promote responsible diving, preservation, and documentation of shipwrecks. The UASC stood ready to take on the *Wells Burt* as a test project, one of the first to document a virgin shipwreck and encourage recreational divers to leave artifacts on the wreck to enhance the experience of fellow divers. Under the leadership of this book's co-author van Heest, the UASC researched the history of the vessel, completed a detailed site plan and photographic inventory of artifacts, published an archaeological report, and designed a traveling exhibit. In 1990, the organization publicized the location, inviting divers to visit the wreck. UASC members made dozens of presentations to area divers, interpreting the history of the *Wells Burt* and encouraging their participation in protecting the wreck. That summer, the *Wells Burt* become the most visited shipwreck in the Chicago area. However, soon thereafter, some diver stole artifacts from the wreck. To add insult to injury, he destroyed an historical marker placed on the wreck by the UASC. As a result, the Illinois Historic Preservation Agency (IHPA) issued the UASC a permit to recover about two dozen loose artifacts that it deemed susceptible to further pilfering. Fortunately, after the UASC conserved and displayed these artifacts, no other artifacts were taken. To this day, the *Wells Burt* continues to rank as one of the most visited shipwrecks in the Chicago area.

Although the "new" schooner A & T had located intrigued Olsen and Lysenko as the *Wells Burt* had, it was not what they were looking for. They recorded the coordinates, and continued their search. Some years later, curiosity got the better of them. They passed the coordinates on to a small group of Chicago area divers who often helped them raise airplanes: Tom Palmisano, Jeff Strunka, Bud Brain, and Bob Schmidt, all of whom took great pleasure in recreational diving and had a particular interest in maritime history. They were excited to have to have the opportunity to be the first divers to visit the wreck.

First Dives on the Wreck

Tom Palmisano was first man down on the wreck on August 1, 2004, and he had been among the first on the *Wells Burt* many years earlier. Jeff Strunka descended right behind him to the level of the deck at about 130 feet. They could clearly see the lake bottom about fifteen feet below them. At first glimpse, they realized immediately that it was in even better condition than the *Wells Burt*. It sits far off Chicago within Illinois state bottomlands on a hard rocky bottom. The depth had protected it from the action of wave and ice movement. Unlike so many other wrecks in the southern area of Lake Michigan, virtually no sand and silt found its way into the hold. Palmisano and the other divers could swim through the interior of the wreck, which, in this case, was devoid of any cargo. Inside they found hundreds of artifacts scattered throughout the forecastle area below the bow and in the stern starboard cargo hold, obviously in the same positions in which they had come to rest after the vessel settled on the bottom. Unlike so many other wrecks in the southern end of Lake Michigan, this one is not embedded in the bottom: It rests squarely on its keel, sitting with only a very slight cant to starboard in the direction in which all three masts had fallen.

At that depth, divers can only spend about five minutes on the bottom without having to decompress. When a diver breathes air under pressure, inert gases, such as nitrogen, dissolve into the body tissues. As the diver ascends, the ambient pressure reduces and the dissolved gases expand. The longer a diver stays on the bottom, the more gas is absorbed and the longer he must spend ascending to allow the gas to come out. If a diver ascends too quickly, decompression sickness can result. Known as the bends, this sickness results from gas bubbles forming in the blood, often in joint areas such as shoulders, wrists, elbows, knees, and ankles. The bubbles can cause extreme pain, often

Since the first dives on the Thomas Hume *visibility has averaged fifty to eighty feet, allowing divers to see more than half of the shipwreck at one glance. The three fallen masts can be seen in this image, looking aft from just under the starboard anchor near the bow. Photograph by Robert Underhill.*

contracting the joints into a bent position (hence the term "the bends"). Without treatment, this condition can be debilitating. In order to accomplish detailed work at 145 feet, a diver would need to spend considerable time there, and, consequently, additional time decompressing during the ascent.

Another problem associated with depth is the effects of nitrogen narcosis caused by breathing compressed nitrogen in deep water. The deeper a diver descends, the more elevated level of confusion he experiences as the pressure of the nitrogen increases. This effect is also called also "Martini's Law" because a diver tends to react about the same way he would after drinking several martinis, a dangerous a state to be in underwater when he must closely monitor his equipment and movements to be safe. Normally, recreational divers limit themselves to 130 feet where the effects of nitrogen narcosis are minimal. To dive deeper than that, many divers obtain advanced training in decompression diving and diving with tri-mix, a gas mixture that reduces the amount of nitrogen and replaces it with helium. Such a mixture in the right percentages can offer the diver a clear head at depth, allowing him to accomplish tasks such as measuring, drawing, photographing, and filming, more safely and with more precision.

Surfacing after his first dive on the new wreck, Strunka started feeling pain in his joints and immediately became concerned that he had suffered a case of the bends. The team had set an anchor near the wreck that landed near a downed mast. Strunka spent most of his dive exploring the stern at a depth level of about 125 feet. As the last diver to ascend, he realized that if his partners pulled the anchor from above, it could become entangled in the mast rigging. Instead, he dived down to the lake bottom at 145 feet to lift and move the anchor to a clearer place, a task putting him deeper for a longer period of time than anticipated. On ascent, the anchor unexpectedly came loose, forcing him to make his decompression stops while adrift, a more difficult undertaking. During that time, he realized he would not have enough gas to make all his necessary decompression stops, and had to surface prematurely. Recognizing the symptoms of the bends, Strunka immediately lay down on the floor of the boat and began breathing oxygen from an emergency tank. His team members notified the Chicago Police Marine Unit while they headed for Chicago. Eighty minutes later, the Chicago Fire Department rushed Strunka to Illinois Masonic Hospital where doctors put him in a hyperbaric chamber for five hours, which brought him down to depth by increasing air pressure and then reducing it slowly to simulate the act of decompression in water. The treatment dissolved any remaining air bubbles and rendered Strunka symptom-free afterwards.

Diving at any depth can be dangerous without proper training and equipment. Diving to this wreck at 145 feet, with the intent to accomplish work, would require advanced diving skills and shipwreck investigation skills. As divers who often worked at depths deeper than this, Palmisano, Strunka, and Schmidt had the right skills. Their fourth partner, 82-year-old Bud Brain, also an experienced diver, provided both guidance and a unique understanding of nineteenth-century schooner design and construction. More than thirty-five years earlier, Brain had been a key member of the team of divers that raised the *Alvin Clark*—a schooner similar to the one they now dived—from 110 feet of water in Green Bay in Lake Michigan. Built in 1847 and lost in a storm in 1864, the *Alvin Clark* had been found in 1967 by a fisherman whose net became entangled in it. Local diver Frank Hoffman retrieved the net and discovered, to his delight, an intact schooner sitting on the lake bottom with its masts still standing. In 1969, after much planning and hundreds of dives, Frank Hoffman, Bud Brain, and a number of other Chicago-area and Wisconsin divers raised the *Clark* from the depths of the lake, pumped it out, and found that it floated on its own. They brought in museum specialists to study the vessel and the hundreds of artifacts still inside, and arranged for it to serve as a museum in Menominee, Michigan. Hundreds of thousands of people flocked to the town over the next two decades to see this schooner brought back from its grave. Although exposure to the elements and lack of funds to conserve the large vessel caused its deterioration and eventual destruction, the world received a glimpse, over more than twenty-five years, of history come alive.[2]

During the balance of the summer of 2004, and periodically over the next two summers, the four Chicago divers made numerous dives to explore, measure, and film the wreck in an attempt to determine its identity. Identifying the wreck would be especially challenging because in the years since the discovery of the *Wells Burt* zebra and quagga mussels, introduced into the Great Lakes from Russia in the ballast water of ocean-going freighters, have colonized on it, as they have on most Great Lakes shipwrecks except those in Lake Superior. Although these filter-feeding mollusks have been single-handedly responsible for the increasing visibility and ambient light penetration, their presence on this wreck obscured any vessel numbers or a name board. The divers would have to brush the mussels off areas where they might find numbers or words, a task that would take many dives due to the limited time allowed for each dive. Initially, they installed a mooring buoy to use to secure the dive boat and eliminate the need to drop anchor, which could possibly damage the vessel. During the next of many dives, they took note of the vessel's construction and deck equipment.

The bowsprit, a long slender spar, extends forward of the vessel's bow. A jib boom is secured to it and extends even farther forward. It would have provided an anchor point for the forestay, a piece of standing rigging that would have kept the foremast from falling backwards. Much of the standing rigging used to tension and support the masts, bowsprit, and jib boom, in this case made of wire, lies on the deck and bottom off the bow's starboard side. Two catheads, large wooden beams located on either side of the bow, angle outward at roughly 45 degrees and would have been used to support the ship's anchors when raising or lowering them, and for carrying the anchor on its stock-end when suspended outside the schooner's side. The catheads served as a sturdy beam to support the massive weight of the anchors, and held the anchor away from the side of the wooden vessel to prevent damage. The starboard anchor rests secured to its mount on the cathead. This older-style anchor has a wooden cross-bar, or stock, that connects to a single metal shank, and two metal arms with sharp flukes. The port anchor, a newer iron-stock style, lies fallen from its cathead and sits upright on the lake bottom. Its anchor chain runs back to the schooner and through the hawser pipe, a metal reinforced hole under the bow through which the anchor chain passed from below the forecastle deck to outside the ship.

Taken using a tripod-mounted camera positioned just forward of the bow on the lake bottom, this image captures the curved bow indicative of the clipper-bow styles popular in Manitowoc, Wisconsin, as well as the iron-stock anchor that may have come loose during the sinking. Photograph by Robert Underhill.

Looking forward from just in front of the foremast, the windlass is seen with the forecastle deck just beyond. Anchor chain could be retrieved using the windlass. A significant amount of chain lies toward the starboard side, and may suggest that the crew had begun to prepare the anchors for lowering just before the accident. Video capture by Jack van Heest.

The forecastle deck, the forwardmost area of the deck, is raised slightly, with gaps between the deck planks that would have allowed cresting water to drain under the feet of the crew. Immediately behind the forecastle sits a sampson post, a large square vertical post used to secure the cable from a tugboat that towed it in rivers or harbors. Sitting up against and behind the tow bit is a large wooden windlass. A horizontal winch, the windlass would have been used to raise the anchors. Just behind it, a small square companionway in the deck allowed crew access below by ladder into the forecastle where they slept. A second opening behind that leads to the forward end of the cargo hold. A bilge pump sits next to the cargo hold opening and a pipe extends down through the cargo hold and into the bilge, a small space under the floor of the vessel. The handle that would have been used to pump up water is missing. On either side of the deck openings are bitts, around which ropes would have been wound to secure the schooner to a dock.

Three hatches, through which cargo would have been loaded, are evenly spaced down the length of the amidships deck. Their covers are gone, probably forced off by air pressure as the vessel sank. The top of the centerboard box is visible through the center hatch. The long, slender box, which housed the centerboard (a retractable keel of sorts) runs from just behind the first hatch to several feet in front of the aft hatch up to the underside of the deck. The centerboard, although not visible, would be inside the box and, when lowered by a winch, would provide lateral stability in the wind while under way but could be retracted upwards into the box when entering shallow water. The box had to be watertight and rise to the level of the deck to prevent water from flooding into the hold. Normally a centerboard winch would be mounted on deck to mechanize the raising of the centerboard. In this case, it is absent, although a hole in the deck just aft of the center hatch and under a large and seemingly heavy boom suggests that it may have been wrenched off during the sinking. In lieu of a winch, tackle on the

Looking aft from just above the windlass, the fallen foremast is visible. Its lower section remains pushed up against the underside of the deck. Mooring bitts can be seen on either side of the hatch access to the forecastle below deck in the lower center. Video capture by Jack van Heest.

boom could have been used to raise and lower the centerboard. Another bilge pump sits near the base of the fallen main mast. Well preserved, it still has the T-shaped handle that would have been pumped up and down to empty the bilge.

All three masts lie toppled to the starboard side. This schooner appears to have been gaff-rigged, also called schooner-rigged, where each sail had a boom below and a gaff above between which the sail was spread, connected to mast hoops that could be pulled up and down the masts to raise or lower the sails. These sails were easy to manipulate,

The main mast (center mast) lies fallen to the starboard side just as the foremast does, having ripped up some of the deck when it fell. Just behind the fallen mast is a bilge pump. Photograph by Robert Underhill.

Looking aft from just over the center hatch, the main mast can be seen fallen toward the starboard side. The top of the centerboard trunk is visible inside the center hatch. Cargo would have been loaded on either side of the centerboard trunk. Video capture by Jack van Heest.

could be handled with a small crew, and allowed flexibility in sailing direction. The top masts, timbers that extended the height of the masts, are broken off the masts and lie scattered on the deck or off the starboard side of the wreck. The foremast, forward of the first hatch, ripped up a few of the deck planks around the mast hole when it fell, as did the main mast between the first two hatches. These masts did not break, but instead fell off their steps on the keel. The bases can be seen pushed up against the underside of the deck. They lie parallel to the lake bottom. Circular wooden rings called mast collars remain around the base of the fore and main masts at deck level and would have helped secure the mast at the deck. Two booms, with crotches, moon-shaped notches at one end that butted up against the mast, lie in the amidships area, one down the center of the deck over the center hatch and the other perpendicular to the deck lying parallel to the main mast, hanging off the starboard side. The aft mast is broken at the level of the cabin floor and the upper portion of the mast fell toward the starboard side like the other masts. Because it is no longer secured to the vessel like the other masts, it lies angled down to the lake bottom where its top has hit the sand. Its broken base remains stepped at the keel and runs up to the underside of the cabin floor. Several gaffs, a portion of a topmast, and remnants of the wire standing rigging lie on the bottom off the starboard side. Any running rigging, used to raise, lower, and position the sails, booms, and gaffs, would have been made of rope and would have deteriorated soon after sinking. There appear to be no mast hoops around the masts, which is curious considering these were very strong rings that could not be removed easily. Deadeyes and chainplates, sets of four each, remain affixed to the outer hull on starboard and port sides. Deadeyes are three-holed, circular wooden blocks that look like a skull. They would have been used to tension the standing rigging that secured the masts. Chainplates are thin strips of metal that held the deadeyes and transferred structural loads to the

Looking forward from above the stern, the floor joists of the cabin can bee seen recessed about four feet lower than the sterncastle deck that surrounds it. The cabin was likely forced off during the sinking. The mizzenmast, now cracked in two, can be seen fallen toward the starboard side. The heavy, cast iron cook stove, once in the cabin, has fallen into the mast hole. Video capture by Jack van Heest.

ship's hull. There is no evidence of canvas sails on board, like on all schooner shipwrecks. The cotton, a vegetable fiber consisting of units of the polymer cellulose, would have deteriorated quickly in the water.[3]

The last quarter of the deck, known as the sterncastle deck, is a raised platform much like the forecastle, accessed by a stair step on port and staboard sides surrounding where the aft deck cabin would have been. Unlike many schooners of the period, this

Looking aft at the stern, the steering gear is apparent inthe center, but the wheel is missing. The posts at either side are bollards around which line would be secured when mooring the vessel at the dock. Video capture by Jack van Heest.

wreck does not have a solid "monkey" rail surrounding the aft deck. Several vertical posts on the port and starboard sides around the sterncastle deck are evidence that the vessel had a rope rail, which would have been threaded through those posts. The cabin obviously came off during the sinking but a small section of its port and starboard walls remain. The floor joists, or "sole" of the cabin, are visible about four feet below the sterncastle deck, but the floor boards are missing. This recessed floor minimized the height of the cabin roof so that the wheelsman could see over the cabin roof when steering. The cabin would have housed

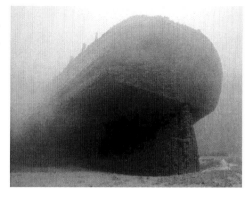

A view from the lake bottom looking toward the stern reveals how the rudder has been forced to the starboard side. The name of the vessel would have been painted across the stern above the waterline, but is now gone. Photograph by Robert Underhill.

the galley, and the cook, captain, and first mate's quarters. The galley's large cast iron cook stove is wedged in the hole in the cabin's floor joints through which the mizzenmast once passed. The lower portion of the mizzenmast has stopped it from falling completely through to the lower deck. The stern is rounded, quite unusual for a schooner, most of which were built with a square stern. The rudderpost and steering gear box sit on the sterncastle farthest aft. The vertical post runs up through the lower hull connecting the rudder to the steering mechanism, a system of gears connected to the wheel that turned the rudder. However, the wheel is missing from this wreck, probably broken off just before or during the sinking. An open hatch is located directly adjacent to the steering mechanism on the starboard side and would have provided one means of access to the lazeret, the storage space under the sterncastle deck and behind the cabin. The rudder sits hard to starboard.

During 2005 the divers took measurements of the wreck, recording the length at about 136 feet from bow to stern, not including the bowsprit, and the width about 25 feet. They also began clearing off zebra mussels from the name board at the starboard side near the stern to see if they could read a name. Some name boards feature carved names, but in this case, the name board undoubtedly had been painted because all they could see was a plain board about eight inches high and six feet wide: any paint long gone due to the scouring action of the silt in the water. In an attempt to find registration numbers, required to be carved into a main beam, they brushed zebra mussels from the beams that surround all the hatch openings, a time-consuming task. Unfortunately, after many dives, they did not find any numbers. In the stern below the deck, they found one item that might offer a clue to the age of the vessel. A bowl lying face down revealed a manufacturer's name: "Royal Ironstone China - Alfred Meakin England." Research indicated that the company began manufacturing plates in 1875. Therefore, the vessel could not possibly have sunk before 1875. That fact combined with the presence of wire rigging—which did not gain widespread use until the 1870s—meant the vessel most certainly sank sometime after the mid-1870s. This information, along with the

Divers cleaned zebra and quagga mussels off the name board located on the starboard side near the stern, but the paint has long since deteriorated. Video capture by Jack van Heest.

measurements, mast configuration, and the fact that it sank without cargo, proved to be the only clues as to the identity.

Tentative Identification

During the winter of 2005-2006, Jeff Strunka led the research efforts. He, like many divers, used an on-line database developed by marine historian David Swayze, who has researched thousands of vessels lost on the Great Lakes. The database can be sorted by name, lake in which the vessel was lost, the cities off which the vessel was lost, ship types, cargo, destination, and year of loss, among other things. As Strunka did various searches with the few bits of data he had, it became obvious that only one schooner lost in Lake Michigan while running light fit the profile.

This revelation, though not conclusive, allowed him to obtain the vessel enrollment documents to see if the information revealed any other details about the schooner that could be compared to the wreck. The Wisconsin Marine Historical Society maintains an archive of thousands of enrollment documents, and Strunka's email and a few dollars got him copies. What he read caused him to rethink his conclusion. The enrollment documents listed the vessel under its original name, *H. C. Albrecht,* a two-masted schooner. Clearly, the wreck on the bottom had three masts. Strunka spent several more days poring through Swayze's database looking for any three-masted schooners lost, even considering vessels recorded as lost in another lake. He knew

An upside down bowl reveals a manufacturer's mark from Alfred Meakin, helping to establish a window of time in which the vessel sailed. Photograph by Robert Underhill.

that contemporary newspapers recorded the three-masted schooner *Cornelia B. Windiate* as lost in Lake Michigan in 1875, but divers found the wreck in Lake Huron.

The discovery of an undated newspaper article in the records of the Lakeshore Museum Center in Muskegon, Michigan, would support his original identification. The article quoted a Captain Drumm, who crewed on the *Albrecht* in 1874. He recalled that the vessel had been built in Manitowoc as a two-mast fore and aft schooner, but "afterwards they added another stick," meaning a third mast. Although the article did not say who added the mast or when that took place, it did indicate that the vessel had been given a different name later in its career. That article gave Strunka confidence that he had identified the wreck correctly. He reported his findings to A & T Recovery and together they contacted the news media to announce their discovery. On September 4, 2005, WBBM News in Chicago interviewed Taras Lysenko, who reported. "Everything's there. It's a time capsule from 114 years ago. It's so intact that even after a century, the masts and rigging are still attached." Although the divers had not found conclusive proof of its identity, Lysenko ventured a hunch for the media. "We have a pretty educated guess that its length matches, its width matches, its depth matches. There's a good chance that it's the *Thomas Hume*."

---

1 http://www.atrecovery.com/athome.htm. November 2010. Interview with Al Olson, February 2011.

2 Thomas Avery. *The Mystery Ship from 19 Fathoms*, (AuTrain, Michigan: Avery Color Studios, 1974), and interviews with Bud Brain 2010.

3 Kellie Marie Gordon, *A Comparative Analysis Of The Deterioration Rates Of Textiles And Their Role In Determining Postmortem Interval*, (Unpublished, The College of William and Mary, May 2003).

A schooner docked at the Hackley & Hume mill in Muskegon, sometime after 1881, sits high above the water awaiting a load of lumber. The possibility exists that the schooner may be the H.C. Albrecht/Thomas Hume, *based on its similarities to the wreck, but the image is not sharp enough to read the name on the stern. The schooner is definitely not the* Rouse Simmons *as previously presumed, because several features do not match known features of that vessel. Lakeshore Museum Center Collection.*

CHAPTER
THREE

Historical Profile
THOMAS HUME

In a roundabout way, the history of the schooner *Thomas Hume* begins with the history of the vessel's birthplace, Manitowoc, Wisconsin, and the confluence of several personalities of that town.

In 1835 the Chicago-based land speculation firm Jones, King & Company formed the Manitowoc Land Company to exploit a large tract of land Jones, King had purchased at the mouth of the Manitowoc River. In July 1837 Benjamin Jones, a principal in Jones, King and a pioneer merchant in Chicago, sailed from Chicago with his family, including his two-year-old son, Alonzo, to establish a homestead at the firm's property on the northwest shore of Lake Michigan.[1] Over the next half-century, Benjamin Jones, generally considered the founder of Manitowoc, established a particularly profitable business in the cutting and milling of lumber. In 1865 Alonzo, after attending a preparatory academy in Connecticut, took over management of his father's lumber and real estate businesses. A few years before Alonzo Jones's birth and an ocean apart, Jasper Hanson was born in Denmark. In 1854 he immigrated to the United States and settled in Manitowoc, already a destination for America-bound Scandinavians, where he became employed at the Benjamin Jones & Company sawmill. Two years later he left Jones for work in the city's burgeoning shipbuilding business, employed by pioneer Manitowoc shipbuilder Greenleaf Rand, and, in 1866, Hanson established his own shipyard near the Jones sawmill with financial backing from Alonzo Jones.[2] Hanson used the extensive knowledge of wooden shipbuilding he had acquired under Rand's tutelage to construct no fewer than thirty-two schooners, steambarges, and tugs over the next twenty-two years. The first three-masted bark *Alice Richards* was launched in November 1867.[3]

The *Richards* had been commissioned by the father of the vessel's namesake, Henry Richards, a frequent investor in Manitowoc-built craft and manager of a thriving Manitowoc machinery shop and iron works founded by his father, Jonah.[4] Hanson contracted with well-known Manitowoc mariner H. C. Albrecht to fit out and rig the vessel during the late winter and early spring of 1867 before Albrecht returned to commanding the Manitowoc schooner *Sea Gem*, owned by Richards. Like Jasper Hanson, Hans Albrecht was a native of Denmark, and had followed the sailing life since the age of ten.[5] As a master he sailed some of Manitowoc's best-known schooners, including the *Jo Vilas* that carried Manitowoc's first direct shipment of grain to Buffalo in 1861. Also like Hanson as his labor on the *Richards*'s rigging indicates, Albrecht engaged in shipyard work during the winter when not sailing, having supervised among other projects the rebuilding of the schooner *John Weber* and the lengthening of the schooner *J & A Stronach*, both during the winter of 1869-70 at Manitowoc.[6] Like many Great Lakes masters, Albrecht used his reputation as a sailor and his own capital to secure partial ownership of several schooners over the years, beginning with the *Jo Vilas* in 1857. Following the 1869 sailing season, Alonzo Jones and Hans Albrecht, born about the same time on different continents but united within Manitowoc's maritime industry, entered into a partnership to construct and operate a new schooner, to be built that winter and ensuing spring by Jasper Hanson and to be commanded by Albrecht. At over one hundred thirty feet in length, the vessel would be the second largest "fore-and-after," or two-masted, schooner ever built at Manitowoc, next to the *Fleetwing*, built in 1867 by Henry Burger, pioneer Manitowoc shipbuilder.[7] To provide a portion of his share of the financing, Albrecht sold back to Jonah Richards the one-third interest Albrecht had purchased two years earlier from Jones in Albrecht's previous command, the *Sea Gem*; Richards in turn sold a quarter-interest in the vessel to Captain Bernhart Schade of Manitowoc, who took command of it for the 1870 sailing season.[8]

Shipbuilding in Manitowoc

Special significance must be given to these early schooners built at Manitowoc, since that northeastern Wisconsin town is generally recognized as the birthplace of the model that evolved into the typical Great Lakes schooner. By the time Jones and Albrecht contracted with Hanson for their schooner, the lake maritime industry considered Manitowoc shipbuilders as the Lakes' preeminent designers and constructors of schooners. Manitowoc's pre-eminence began when Stephen Bates, a Canadian-born shipwright, traveled to the American Midwest from Maine in the 1840s to seek a new market for his shipbuilding skills, and settled at Manitowoc in 1851.[9] Bates's son, William, studied with innovative American naval architect John Willis Griffiths at his school of naval architecture at New York in the mid-1840s. Griffiths, like the younger Bates the son of a skilled shipwright, emerged at a young age as the nineteenth century's leading American naval architect. He was best known for his development of the "clipper" style of sailing ship design, realized in his design for the China tea clipper *Rainbow* launched at New York in 1845, the first of its type and revolutionary for the era.[10] The younger Bates split his time between Manitowoc, working at his father's shipyard, and New York and elsewhere, immersing himself in the study of naval architecture and issues related to America's maritime industry, toiling in shipyards from Chicago to Louisville. In 1849 William Bates returned to Manitowoc and applied what he had learned from Griffiths to the design and construction of a radical new sailing vessel built at the Bates yard, the *Challenge*, launched in 1852.[11]

The *Challenge*, like Griffiths's clippers, had its origins in small sailing vessels built a hundred years earlier in Colonial America that came to be known as "Baltimore clippers." These vessels had a relatively small draft, which allowed them entry into shoal waters inaccessible by typical full-keeled vessels. To compensate for the lack of keel while sailing, a centerboard was lowered to maintain the vessel's balance. Also, the clippers had relatively sharp prows and sterns and narrow beams, which made them speedy sailers. All these factors, combined with the typical and efficient brigantine rig then in use on the Great Lakes and the flat bottom Bates gave the vessel to increase its cargo capacity, made the *Challenge* a phenomenon of the day. It proved to be a quick, easily manageable vessel that could dock in shallow water, a vessel ideally suited to the demands of the burgeoning lumber industry that surrounded the shores of Lake Michigan.[12] Quickly, the *Challenge* became the model for virtually all subsequent Great Lakes schooners. Manitowoc became so identified with this advance in schooner design that the town informally adopted the slogan "Clipper City," immortalized with the launching at the Bates yard in spring 1854 of a hundred-foot schooner of that name.[13] William Bates would leave Manitowoc in 1854 for New York to found and edit, with Griffiths, a periodical devoted to maritime matters, *The Nautical Magazine and Navy Journal*, while designing vessels for saltwater, returning intermittently to Manitowoc. In 1864 the Bates family sold the Manitowoc shipyard to Greenleaf Rand, employer of Jasper Hanson, and moved operations to Chicago, that later shipyard being destroyed in the Great Fire of 1871. William Bates left shipbuilding but remained prominent in the American maritime industry, becoming Commissioner of Navigation within the Treasury Department, 1889-1892, under President William Henry Harrison.[14] The last vessel built by the Bates family at Manitowoc, the *Sea Gem*, was under Hans Albrecht's command when Albrecht and Jones contracted for their new schooner.

Building a wooden ship by manual labor, as was done in the shipyards of Manitowoc and elsewhere on the Great Lakes during the nineteenth century, is a remarkably complex and arduous task. Although the Jones sawmill could provide planking in various lengths, widths, and thicknesses, cut using its steam-powered circular saws, and the Richards foundry could provide iron fittings, for the most part a vessel would be hand wrought. The Hanson yard was located on the Manitowoc River at what had come to be known as "Shipyard Point" at the end of Buffalo Street next to the sawmill just west of downtown Manitowoc. This proved a convenient location because it had direct access to the mill's product and a relatively flat piece of land next to sheltered water at the northerly bend of the river on which to build.[15] Typically, a substantial proportion of the building crew would be sailors home for the winter who, in addition to having intimate knowledge of the typical schooner's construction, had additional carpentry, caulking, or rigging skills acquired while sailing. Ship construction during the winter offered other seasonal laborers, from farmers to granary workers, to house and barn carpenters, an income during the cold months. Manitowoc's location served to provide the material of the shipbuilding process, too. It sat near huge tracts of pine and, significantly, at the edge of stands of white oak that extended through Wisconsin from the Mississippi to Green Bay, white oak the essential ingredient in shipbuilding in the nineteenth century.[16]

Building the *H. C. Albrecht*

Most likely, the construction of the schooner for Albrecht and Jones began in the late fall of 1869.[17] Workers would have laid out on the building site, close to the Manitowoc River, large, rectangular blocks of oak upon which the vessel's keel would sit.

The blocks would be adjusted vertically for the span of the keel's length to provide a straight and level foundation for the craft. Apart from the vertical hull framing and stem- and sternposts, "plumb and level" were carpentry terms that didn't apply to shipwrights, because of the curves and sheer of the typical vessel. A white oak timber of around ten by twenty inches thickness and of a single piece conforming to the keel's length was placed upon the keel blocks. To the keel would be bolted the oak ribs, or "frames," of the hull, each rib ranging from about fourteen inches in depth next to the keel and tapering to about ten inches at the top of the rib, where it would form the structure for the bulwark around the main deck. Generally, the ribs would be set around one to two feet apart. From fore to aft, the shape of each rib changed to conform to the model of the hull, with those forward and aft, being narrower at the keel than those amidships, reflecting the lines of the vessel's bow and stern. The ribs themselves were composed of several pieces of oak, laboriously crafted to adhere to the hull's shape, then fitted, glued, and bolted together. The vessel's stem would be constructed in the same manner of several pieces that followed the form of the ship's prow, and bolted to the stempost. Atop the lowest plane of the ribs and extending the length of the keel would be bolted the main keelson, around six inches in thickness, yet another substantial oak member to reinforce the structure of the keel, the vessel's literal backbone. On either side of the keelson, just before where the ribs curved upwards to form the vessel's sides, would be bolted two more pieces of white oak the entire length of the keel, side keelsons, to further reinforce the structural integrity of the base of the vessel's hull. The ribs would be placed beginning in the middle and working to the bow and stern, where vertical stem- and sternposts of heavy white oak timbers were erected.

Because the schooners of the Great Lakes carried centerboards, a design advance promoted by Bates and used by the first Manitowoc "clippers," these vessels actually had "holes" in the bottoms of their hulls, an aperture around ten inches wide and extending roughly a third of the keel's length and to the immediate starboard of the keel where the starboard keelson would be. Through this slot was lowered the centerboard. The starboard side of the vessel's ribs adjacent to the centerboard slot, obviously, could not extend as a continuous piece, so the ends of those ribs where they met the centerboard slot were set about six inches into a frame called a sole piece. To compensate for the lack of continuous framing and the missing section of starboard keelson at this point, an additional keelson was placed above the sole piece and an additional "top rider" keelson atop the port keelson running the length of the keel, all to strengthen the hull about the centerboard slot. A large box, the centerboard trunk, housed the centerboard, running from the floor of the hold to the underside of the top deck, constructed of substantial framing upon which were bolted caulked planks providing a relatively watertight enclosure for the centerboard. The centerboard itself consisted of oak planks doweled and glued side-by-side forming a long, flat slab. An iron rod at the forward end of the trunk provided a pivot point at which the centerboard could be raised or lowered, using a chain or cable connected to the board's lower aft corner running upwards to a winch on deck.

With the vessel's keel and ribs in place, beams of a gentle arch would be placed across the vessel connecting the ribs to form the foundation of the main deck. Then, the arduous task of planking the hull, outside and inside, began. Also of white oak, the inboard side of each plank had to be carefully fitted to the curve of the ribs it covered and bent to conform to the narrowing of the ribs toward the bow and stern. Skilled craftsmen accomplished this by hand using axes, adzes (axes with their blades at right angles to their handles), and wood planes. Additionally, each continuous strip, or "strake," of planking constantly changed in width, since the concave nature of the hull toward the stem and stern necessitated progressively thinner widths of planking so that a uniform and horizontal strake could be maintained. This required laborious measuring, fitting, and cutting by the ship carpenters. To bend the planks to conform to the hull's shape, "steam boxes" were used, the steam opening the grain of the tough oak sufficiently so that a plank could be bent by cable or clamp against the ribs for bolting. The bolting of the hull planks consisted of driving the bolts through the planks and into holes slightly smaller than the diameter of the bolts, previously drilled by hand in the ribs. Meanwhile, the inboard sides of the planks butted against each other perfectly tight, but the outside edges were beveled leaving an outside gap of around a quarter inch. Into this gap with mallets and chisels would be driven strands of hemp, generally old rope, soaked in pine tar, called "oakum," which would caulk the seams. Then hot pitch would be applied, making the seams watertight. This process would be replicated continually in maintaining the vessel's hull throughout its life. After the hull had been planked but before caulking, skilled shipwrights used adzes to provide a smooth outside finish to the hull, which would be further worked using hand planes. The deck planking consisted of white pine four inches thick, around six inches wide, and ranging in length up to thirty or more feet, connected to the deck beams and caulked just as the oak hull planking was to the ribs. The interior of the hull was planked with white oak ranging from four to five inches in thickness, the oak used to withstand the abuse the hold would take from the various cargoes to be carried, coal and ore in particular.

Most likely the work on the new vessel for Albrecht and Jones was done during the fall, so that, as in house building, a relatively weathertight structure would protect workers during the bitterly cold Wisconsin winter while the vessel's interior and cabins were constructed. By the end of March 1870, the *Manitowoc Pilot* reported that the new vessel's "spars were up," and that it would be launched once the winter ice left the harbor.[18] The reporter for the *Pilot* probably meant that the schooner's two masts had been "stepped," or put in place. Stepping the mast consisted of using block and tackle to raise the mast in place through an opening in the main deck and into the mast's "step," an oak timber affixed across the keelson into which the mast's bottom, or "heel," was placed. Into the timber was carved a mortice into which fitted a tenon cut into the heel of the mast. Where the masts pierced the deck special stiffening members ran beneath the deck from between the beams and from the ribs to a frame containing the mast. Around the mast and below the fife rail that enclosed the mast on deck was oak, rather than pine, planking, to further reinforce the area around the mast. Straight white pine logs two feet or more in diameter and over a hundred feet long formed the masts. The logs would be squared at the sawmill after which carpenters would progressively make them eight-cornered, sixteen-cornered, and so on, using draw knives and spokeshaves until the logs were sufficiently rounded to be finished with hand planes. As the diameter of the log was being rounded into a mast, its length during the same process was tapered from the heel to top. Shipwrights formed a vessel's bowsprit and booms. After the masts were set and with the booms that spread the sails in place, the shipriggers went about the difficult chore of assembling the new vessel's complex "cordage," its rigging system. Most likely, Captain Albrecht supervised this task. Cordage consisted of "standing" rigging and "running" rigging. The standing rigging, the various stays and shrouds that remain stationary during sailing (such as the lines that run from the vessel's sides to the top of a mast to provide its lateral support) would be put in place first. Generally on the Great Lakes in 1870, this consisted of hemp rope soaked in pine tar to prevent weathering. However, Albrecht and Jones's schooner represented an innovation among Manitowoc's already progressive shipbuilders. It was the first vessel built at that port to use metal wire rather than rope for its standing rigging, a much stronger material and, especially when coated with oil or tar, even more resistant to the effects of weather.[19] After the standing rigging was in place, the riggers completed the complicated running riggings, all the various halyards, sheets, and other lines generally made of untreated Manila rope and their various tackle that control the sails while the vessel is in operation. Meanwhile, carpenters and joiners completed the vessel's interior and cabin while mechanics installed the craft's various auxiliaries, including capstan, windlass, and its steering gear, among other devices. The masts before stepping had already received paint at those few stretches where the mast rings, which connected the sails to the mast, did not touch, while that area received several coats of spar varnish to insure a smooth finish to facilitate the raising of the sails. The hulls of most schooners of the day at Manitowoc, as elsewhere on the Lakes, received a white hull, as probably did Albrecht and Jones's vessel. Below the waterline "Stockholm tar," pine pitch distilled from the slow-burning of pine lumber (plentiful as waste from the sawmills of Manitowoc), combined with linseed oil to make the pitch brushable, made the hull even more watertight, in addition to the oakum in the hull seams. During construction coarse salt had been added in between the ribs and planking to prevent dry rot, a process that would be repeated over the first three or four years of the vessel's life to protect the wood.

At Manitowoc as elsewhere on the Lakes, schooners were generally in a virtually completed state when launched, and, because of the constricted channels on the Lakes, generally launched sideways. Launching consisted of placing heavy wooden beams between the keel blocks, which were supported on the side of the vessel away from the water by timbers, allowing an angled, gravity-induced entry into the water. During most launches *circa* 1870, wooden wedges were placed between the timbers and the beams, the tops of which were coated with tallow or grease. The wedges would be rhythmically pounded by shipyard workers wielding sledgehammers until the beams lifted the vessel off the blocks and the vessel slid onto the greased beams and into the water. Jack screws beneath the ends of the beams could accomplish the same result. It is not known what method was used with Albrecht and Jones's schooner, but it was successfully launched on Saturday, April 16, 1870, christened *H. C. Albrecht*, in honor of her master and part-owner.[20] As testimony to the vessel's nearly completed state upon launch, the *H. C. Albrecht* made its maiden voyage on Monday, May 2, 1870, little more than two weeks after it entered the Manitowoc River, heading around the tip of Door County and into Green Bay to load lumber at Menominee, Michigan, for Chicago.[21]

H. C. Albrecht's **Career in Manitowoc**

It would seem likely that the *Albrecht's* first cargo would define the vessel's working life, given the centrality of the Great Lakes lumber trade of that era, but this was not exclusively the case for the first few years of the schooner's life. Most likely, Albrecht and Jones had an eye on the burgeoning grain trade on the Lakes, since the *Albrecht* had been designed to carry 16,000 bushels, a relatively large capacity for a vessel its size and so remarked upon by the *Manitowoc Pilot* two months after its launching.[22] By 1870 the grain trade, mostly wheat and rye, had already begun to supersede lumber as Manitowoc's leading waterborne export, totaling over 500,000 bushels annually by the year the *Albrecht* entered service.[23] Indeed, from what little that can be pieced together about the *Albrecht's* voyages in the several years following its construction, it appears Captain Albrecht initially concentrated on the grain trade, especially Chicago to Buffalo with return trips of coal loaded at Buffalo or Cleveland, as well as running up to Lake Superior in the ore trade and cargoes of Chicago corn for Goderich, Ontario, while also maintaining typical Lake Michigan lumber runs, primarily from Menominee to Chicago and Michigan City, Indiana.[24] However, near the end of the *Albrecht's* second season on the lakes, the blaze that consumed a good portion of the burgeoning metropolis of Chicago in 1871 altered the nature of the lumber trade on Lake Michigan and affected the career of the *Albrecht*. By the time of the Great Chicago Fire, Chicago with its central location and transportation facilities had already become the nation's leading lumber market, with over a hundred lumber yards handling over a billion board feet annually, mostly from Wisconsin and Michigan.[25] Following the fire there arose a sudden huge demand for pine not only to rebuild the city itself, but to slake the rapidly growing demand for lumber to the West, recently opened to high-speed transportation by the completion of the transcontinental railroad several years earlier. By 1892, the peak of the Chicago lumber trade, that city's lumber wholesalers would sell 2.25 billion board feet, or a quarter of all pine harvested in the lower lake region.[26] As a result, lumbering flourished, especially on the east shore of Lake Michigan from Muskegon to Petoskey, and demand grew for vessels to carry Michigan pine to Chicago. Jones and Albrecht apparently believed this a favorable time at which to put the *H. C. Albrecht* on the market and plan to build an even larger craft to capitalize upon the scarcity of bottoms and the probable increase in freight rates that scarcity would bring. In February 1873 the *Manitowoc Pilot* announced that Jones and Albrecht had sold the vessel for $17,500 and would "immediately commence building a more expensive and commodious one to cost $30 to $35 thousand," which is precisely what they did. They contracted with Henry Burger to build a 173-foot, three-masted schooner, the *C. C. Barnes*, named in honor of the president of the First National Bank of Manitowoc and launched September 27, 1873, again commanded by Hans Albrecht.[27] However, the initial sale didn't materialize, and the *Albrecht* did not find a buyer until

December. Just forty-two months after the *Albrecht* had slid sideways into the Manitowoc River, its owners sold the vessel to a party in Chicago. Hans Albrecht would command the *C. C. Barnes* primarily in the cross-lake grain trade until 1890 when he sold it and took command of the steam barge *T. S. Christie*, in which he owned an interest. Hans Albrecht retired four years later, and died at Manitowoc March 30, 1906.[28]

H. C. Albrecht's Career in Chicago

On January 24, 1873, Alonzo Jones and Hans Albrecht sold the *H. C. Albrecht* to Captain William Walsh of Chicago for $15,500.[29] Walsh's background mirrored that of most of the other personages involved with the construction and ownership of the vessel to that point, an immigrant who had headed to sea at a very young age. Born in County Wexford, Ireland, in 1829, he shipped out as a cabin boy on an Irish schooner in the Irish and Baltic Seas trade at the age of fourteen and the next year apprenticed himself to an Irish ship owner. Over the next quarter-century he gained extensive seagoing experience on saltwater sailing brigs and barks between North America and Britain, and by 1853 he was engaged in steamboating on the Tombigbee and Alabama Rivers. In 1854 he found work as a shiprigger at New York City, and opened a grocery business at that city. Following that venture's failure, Walsh returned to sailing, shipping out as a mate on schooners out of Buffalo. By 1859 he had become master of the twelve-year-old schooner *H. N. Gates*, and the next year began investing in sailing craft, just as Hans Albrecht had, purchasing a third interest in the relatively new schooner *Barney Eaton*, which he also commanded. Over the next dozen years Walsh, who had settled in Chicago in 1855, invested in four schooners, including the *Peoria*, which he sold in order to finance his purchase of the *Albrecht*.[30] Walsh commanded the *Albrecht* for the next five years. It is difficult to ascertain exactly in what primary trade the vessel engaged, but evidence from the daily Chicago newspapers suggests that Walsh concentrated on bringing lumber to Chicago, especially from Ford River, Michigan, just south of Escanaba, as well as Muskegon and even Alpena on the Lake Huron side of Michigan.[31] Walsh's subsequent duties after owning and commanding the *Albrecht* indicate that, perhaps, the Ford River trade occupied much of the *Albrecht's* service, since Walsh partnered with the Ford River Lumber Company in the ownership of two schooners, *Resumption* and *Ford River*, the construction of which he oversaw at Milwaukee in 1878-1879 and which he managed for the lumber firm. Walsh also commanded the *Ford River* until his retirement from sailing in 1881.[32] Walsh remained active in vessel ownership, and in 1889 he had Burger & Burger construct the three-masted schooner *Cora A,* the very last sailing vessel built at Manitowoc, bringing to an end the city's succession of "clippers."[33]

Walsh had owned and sailed the *Albrecht* during a particularly troubling financial period, following the Panic of 1873 and for most of the six-year depression that followed. During this time lumber production in Michigan, including the Muskegon River area, remained flat. However, as the economy began to recover the Muskegon mills and others in the region began to witness renewed demand for their product. Lumber production at Muskegon more than doubled between 1875 and 1879, but the number of sawmills operating in central Michigan had begun a precipitous decline beginning in 1873 with the Panic, indicating that fewer but larger mills were beginning to dominate the production of pine.[34] In Muskegon, the firm of Hackley & McGordon emerged as one of the largest of these dominant mills. The company did so by following a pattern of constrained vertical integration, controlling the production of its lumber by owning its own timberlands and mill and controlling the transportation of its logs to market. Hackley & McGordon purchased the *H. C. Albrecht* in 1878 to add to its growing fleet of vessels to transport its product to market.

Sale of the *H. C. Albrecht* to Hackley & McGordon

In 1859 with his father, Joseph, and another partner, Charles Hackley purchased a bankrupt lumber mill in Muskegon, Michigan, a victim of the Panic of 1857, and within four decades expanded that holding into one of the largest lumber operations in the Midwest.[35] Joseph Hackley, a carpenter and contractor, had left his home in Southport, Wisconsin (Kenosha today), to find work among the proliferating lumber mills of Muskegon, and encouraged his son to join him. Charles did so by working for his passage across the lake in the spring of 1856 on the schooner *Challenge*, the first of William Bates's Manitowoc "clippers." Hackley hired a laborer to work in the mill, James McGordon, but within two years, based upon his skills and talents in the lumbering enterprise, McGordon emerged as a partner in the firm of Hackley & McGordon.[36] Hackley & McGordon sought to rationalize the production of white pine lumber by controlling as many steps in that production as possible. In addition to owning the sawmill, the company purchased the land on which the raw material grew, devising an efficient milling system to which contracted loggers would deliver the pine. Beginning in the 1870s, the firm began relying upon its own vessels to deliver the product to what was by far and away its largest market, Chicago.

The availability of suitable vessels to carry lumber to Chicago and the freight rates charged by those vessels vacillated as the Chicago lumber market boomed in the 1870s. To insure transportation of its product to Chicago and to avoid the volatility of freight charges (and to extract even more marginal profit into its lumber enterprise), Hackley & McGordon began purchasing the firm's own schooners, beginning with the *Z. G. Simmons* and *Rouse Simmons* early in the decade.[37] Between 1871 and 1898 the firm would own seven schooners, exclusively employed in the Muskegon-Chicago lumber trade and carrying the partnership's lumber. To assist its vessels and others into the harbor at Muskegon, Hackley & McGordon had built in 1874 and 1876, respectively, the tugs *J. H. Hackley* and *James McGordon*. Because of cutthroat competition among independent tug operators at Muskegon and other lumber ports on the east shore, this proved an unprofitable enterprise, and the firm sold the two tugs by 1878. In fact, Hackley & McGordon acquired the *Albrecht* from William Walsh through a partial trade of the *Hackley*.[38] Between 1875 and 1880 the Muskegon lumbering region experienced a surge in production, doubling to almost a half billion board feet of pine.[39] Hackley & McGordon led this surge, and undoubtedly its purchase of the *H. C. Albrecht* in 1878 was directly tied to increased demand at Chicago and the associated increase in production at the Muskegon mill.

Masters of the *H. C. Albrecht*

During its first years with Hackley & McGordon, Simon O'Day of Muskegon commanded the *Albrecht*. O'Day, like Walsh, had emigrated from Ireland and took to sailing the Great Lakes at the age of sixteen, eventually becoming master of the schooner *Contest* of Chicago at the age of twenty-nine. Like Hans Albrecht, O'Day seemed to realize that the days of the schooner were numbered, and in 1881 he gave up command of the *Albrecht* and purchased an interest in the eight-year-old steam barge *C. Hickox*, one of a succession of steam craft he would command and partially own over the next two decades.[40] In 1882 Chicagoan Christian E. Baker became master of the vessel.[41] These two captains shared a curious distinction, both being cited by the United States Patent Office as holders of patents. A Muskegon inventor in 1893 assigned two-thirds of his patent for an automatic railway crossing gate to O'Day and several other Muskegon residents.[42] Three years later the Patent Office awarded O'Day his own patent for a projectile to be used to dispense "storm oil" to quell high seas.[43] In 1885 Baker received a patent for a new type of ship's propeller consisting of a continuous tread of air-filled cylinders that rest upon the water's surface.[44] Previously, in 1883, Baker invented a new type of fire escape and assigned half the invention to fellow Hackley captain Charles Eggert.[45] Chicagoan Harry Albrightson took command of the vessel by around 1890 and would be its final master, but he seems to have not had the inventive bent of his predecessors.[46]

Thomas Hume and the Firm of Hackley & Hume

With the death of James McGordon in 1880, Hackley dissolved the partnership and formed a new one with the former firm's chief bookkeeper, thirty-three-year-old Thomas Hume, under the name Hackley & Hume.[47] Hume had worked for Hackley for the previous eight years and Hackley had found him to be a talented and faithful employee.

Thomas Hume began his life on June 15, 1848, in Beechfield, County Down, Ireland, the second child and oldest son to William Hume and Mary Ann Bailie Hume, and was named after his father's father, Thomas Finley Hume. Though William had as bright a mind as any of his brothers, he worked on the family farm helping his brothers to gain an education so that they could advance beyond farming, becoming clergymen, a doctor, and a merchant. William would sacrifice for his son's education as well. Thomas attended a Moravian school when young and then his father placed him with his Uncle Thomas, a merchant in Belfast to learn his trade and attend the Royal Belfast Academical Institution. There, he met another young man who also happened to be named Tommy, apprenticing from his home in Scotland. The boys became fast friends but Tommy was so homesick he convinced young Hume to sneak off on a train for Scotland; the police caught the boys and sent them back to Belfast. Angered by his son's straying, William Hume sent Thomas to another uncle, Rev. Abraham Hume in Liverpool, so that he could receive education for the diplomatic service, in preparation for financial work in China.[48]

Life in Liverpool under a controlling uncle with no other children around soon became intolerable for young Hume and he wrote his mother begging her to bring him home. Although this created a terrible rift between William and Abraham, she relented. Sadly, just a short time after returning home, Hume's mother died, leaving the young boy in the care of his father and his older sister, Margaret, who helped out with the children. In time young Hume's material grandmother helped him get an apprenticeship at Stevenson and Aiken, a firm of wholesale and retail grocers and hardware merchants in Dungannon. His father signed a six-year contract releasing the fourteen-year-old boy into indentured servitude with John Stevenson beginning on November 1, 1862. Terms of the contract provide insight into the strict condition Thomas would spend during his teen years: "He shall faithfully serve his Master, his secrets keep, his lawful command everywhere gladly do. He shall not contract Matrimony within the said term. He shall not play Cards, Dice, Tables nor any other unlawful games. He shall

Thomas Hume soon after he became Charles Hackley's partner in 1881. Lakeshore Museum Center Collection.

not haunt, nor use Taverns, Ale-houses, nor Play-houses, nor absent himself from his said Master's service day or night…." In return Stevenson promised to teach and instruct, "by the best way and means he can, in the same art he useth," providing meat, drink and lodging and all other necessaries befitting such an apprentice.[49]

Despite these seemingly tough conditions, young Hume found he was good at the work and it interested him. Even before his term of servitude ended, Stevenson and Aiken offered him a paid position in January 1867 as a cashier and manager of the wholesale department, which he served faithfully for the next three years. Aiken provided Hume, then twenty-two years old, with a letter of referral to take with him to America, his next destination. Aiken particularly noted his excellent moral character, a hallmark Hume would carry with him for the balance of his life.[50]

Since 1867 when Hume met his Uncle James Bailie's wife, who had come to Ireland from America to visit after her husband's death, Hume had developed an interest in going to America. In the spring of 1870 he carried Aiken's reference letter with him as he traveled to Marshall, Michigan, where Mrs. Bailie had been living with her parents on a farm. Mrs. Bailie's brother, John Banks, directed Hume to Muskegon, which he thought would be a good place where a young man of ambition might succeed. Hume took a position in a grocery store, but did not get along with the owner and so he began to learn how to tally lumber. His aptitude for mathematics shone, but all the positions had already been filled that summer and he could only find work when a large fleet came into port.

Charles Hackley, an already established and successful lumberman, saw in young Thomas Hume the qualities he wished in a partner: financial aptitude, honesty, and integrity. Lakeshore Museum Center Collection.

In the winter of 1870-1871 he took a job scaling logs in the woods though he had at that time little ability to even differentiate a pine tree from an oak. The next summer Hume received a permanent position tallying lumber at Bluffton, and in winter again scaling logs, following this routine each year through 1872, all the while getting to know Mrs. Bailie's sister, Margaret Ann Banks.

In the summer of 1873, Charles Hackley began seeking a bookkeeper for his businesses. He had seen the tally work of a young Irish man, Thomas Hume, and began inquiring of this man's whereabouts to offer him a job. Tracking him down in Port Sherman, Hackley offered him a position in the fall of 1872, but Hume had already committed to work scaling logs for a Mr. Wilcox and did not feel right in breaking his contract. Hackley must have respected that Hume would not give up even a low-level job for a much loftier position because he had given Wilcox his word, and so Hackley spoke with Wilcox personally and made arrangements to secure Hume's service. In November, Hume became the bookkeeper for the firms of Hackley & McGordon and H. H. Hackley and Sons.

Upon beginning his career with Charles Hackley in November 1872, Hume settled into a home in Muskegon and married Margaret Ann Banks on January 22, 1873. Less than a year later Margaret gave birth to the couple's first daughter whom they named Margaret, probably as much for Hume's beloved sister, Margaret, as for the child's own mother. Over the next fifteen years the couple had six more children, one about every two or three years including Helen, Ann, George, Florence, Constance, and finally Thomas Hackley in 1888. Young Thomas's middle name showed the love and respect that Hume had developed for the man who had become his lifelong friend.

Since 1873, Hackley had watched Hume with great interest and saw that in the rough, wild town of Muskegon this young man operated with well-founded principles, a good religious commitment, and a love for home and family. Hume believed that a man's word was as good as his bond and was always good to his word. Hackley trusted him implicitly, increasing his salary and responsibility over the years. Upon the death of his partner McGordon, Hackley could think of no better person to fill McGordon's shoes than Thomas Hume.[51]

Hackley had papers drawn up in June 1881 to establish the new lumbering and vessel partnership, with Hackley contributing three-quarters of the capital for the

Thomas Hume began his career in Michigan as a scaler, a man who tabulates the board feet of lumber that a log will yield. Lakeshore Museum Center Collection.

business. Hume did not have the money to buy out McGordon's heirs, so Hackley bought it, with Hume insuring his life for the payment.[52] Coinciding with that new partnership, on June 18, 1881, Hume acquired McGordon's one-quarter interest in the schooner *H. C. Albrecht* and steam tug *James McGordon* and the company surrendered earlier enrollments and re-enrolled the vessels under new ownership.[53]

The *H.C. Albrecht/Thomas Hume*'s **Career in Michigan**

The *Albrecht*'s service under both partnerships' ownership consisted exclusively of transporting the firm's pine to Chicago and returning empty to Muskegon. At Chicago, Hackley had entered into a very close business arrangement with Benjamin Franklin Deming, whose father had been a partner with one of Hackley's early employers and mentors, pioneer Muskegon lumberman Gideon Truesdell.[54] Deming & Company operated a yard in the Chicago lumber district centered around 22nd and Halsted Streets at 236 South Water Street, an almost five-mile tow by steam tug for a schooner from Lake Michigan up the South Branch of the Chicago River. An immense sprawl of slips, wharves, and warehouses, the area served as the wholesale lumber market for a good portion of the nation, handling a quarter of all the pine grown in the Great Lakes region.[55] Despite Chicago's preeminence as a railway hub, during the 1880s over 90 percent of this pine arrived at Chicago by water aboard schooners or, increasingly common, steam vessels, which were beginning to replace the wind-driven craft.[56] Over the next dozen years the *Albrecht* (renamed *Thomas Hume* in March 1884 after major

Hackley & Hume felled the first stands of pine nearest the Muskegon River. Lumberjacks stacked logs on the river banks, then sent them floating downstream to the mills. Lakeshore Museum Center Collection.

repairs during the winter) carried lumber consigned for Deming and twenty-one other lumber yards clustered along the South Branch, including some of the biggest wholesalers in the trade such as the Soper Lumber Company and the S. K. Martin Lumber Company.[57] The vessel's first trip for its new owners occurred when the *Albrecht* left Muskegon on Thursday, April 18, 1878, with almost a quarter-million board feet of pine, consigned to Deming & Company and cut from Hackley & McGordon's logs.[58] It is interesting to note that the *Albrecht* (and assumingly, the firm's other schooners) did not carry exclusively for the Hackley interests. Over the schooner's remaining career, Hackley's account books show that it carried lumber to Chicago for some of Hackley's biggest competitors in Muskegon, including Blodgett & Byrne, Beidler Manufacturing Company, A. V. Mann & Company, and other mills.[59] At Chicago, in addition to being a frequent purchaser of Hackley & Hume's lumber, Deming also collected payments on the firm's behalf from consignees of the lumber and functioned as its agent for its vessels.[60]

On average, it appears the *Thomas Hume* carried, per trip, around 260,000 board feet of lumber.[61] Hackley & McGordon and later Hackley & Hume made it a policy to sell "seasoned" rather than the heavier "green" lumber, insufficiently dried from the logs' immersion in Muskegon River and Lake on their way to the mill. Seasoned lumber being less dense, the *Hume* and the firm's other schooners could carry more board feet of it per trip relative to green lumber. At the mill, the firm negotiated with the local, somewhat informally organized Muskegon lumber handlers' union (the "dock wallopers") on a price for the strenuous loading of the lumber cargo, both in the hold and on deck. After 1877 at Chicago a far more organized and powerful group, the Lumber Vessel Unloaders' Union (also known as the "Lumber Shovers"), controlled the unloading of vessels at

Throughout the cold months, lumberjacks cut trees and "banked" the logs in piles until the spring warm-up broke up the river ice and logs could be floated downriver to the mills. Lakeshore Museum Center Collection.

that port. Payments to the dock wallopers were initially based on a daily rate, but by the twentieth century the labor rate became based upon the actual board feet loaded or unloaded. By 1906 that rate was $0.60 per thousand board feet of pine at Chicago. A union representative would collect the total labor charge from the vessel captain and divide it among the wallopers, their gang boss, and the union. That cost would be deducted as part of the lumber's shipping cost.[62] Chicago was also home to the Lake Seamen's Union founded there in 1863, which, amalgamated with the National Union of Seaman of America in 1892, had union halls scattered among the most major Great Lakes ports and by the late 1870s set a *per diem* rate for seamen's wages.[63] If one were to correlate the various expenses incurred by the *Thomas Hume* on a typical round trip between Chicago and Muskegon with the cost of delivering the lumber, a vague idea of the profitability of Hackley & Hume's fleet arises. To take a representative year, 1883, the *Hume* (as the *H. C. Albrecht*) made only twenty-one round trips to Chicago from Muskegon, carrying on average 225,398 board feet of pine. [64] Hackley records indicate the captain was paid around $1800 for that season, or an average of $85.71 per trip, and that the vessel normally carried six crew members.[65] Although labor rates fluctuated during any given year, that season, from what evidence exists, it appears the Lake Seamen's Union mandated a $2.00 *per diem* pay scale during several months, which would yield a wage of $48 for the entire crew for a typical four days of sailing.[66] Therefore, per trip the direct sailing labor costs amounted to around $133. This does not take into account the probability that a first mate likely received higher wages than a deckhand. At the beginning of the 1883 season, the going rate for shipping lumber from Muskegon to Chicago amounted to $1.59 per thousand board feet; assuming Hackley & Hume

Once the floating logs reached Lake Muskegon, "boomers" directed them to the various mills where they were sawn into lumber and piled at the dock to dry and await shipment. Hackley & Humes mill was located on the north side of Lake Muskegon as seen in this photo dated sometime after 1881 when Hackley and Hume became partners. As noted on page 38, there remains a possibility the schooner at the dock is the Albrecht/Hume. *Lakeshore Museum Center Collection.*

charged that rate to its wholesale customers for its lumber delivered at Chicago, it seems the typical voyage of the *Albrecht* during the 1883 season grossed around $358 in revenue.[67] Of course, a large expense virtually all vessels calling at Chicago incurred would be towage fees, and especially so for unpowered lumber schooners that had to make the trek far down the South Branch of the Chicago River to unload and back to the lake. It is very difficult today to determine what those charges would have been in 1883, but it is known that in 1901 the typical vessel paid $100 to $160 to tug operators for round-trip towing down and up the Chicago River and in 1907 a typical 2,000-ton steamer paid vessel paid between $100 and $150.[68] It is difficult to ascertain what the towage fees were that the *Albrecht* may have encountered in 1883 since those fees proved a function of the fluctuating greed of the Chicago Tug Owners' Protective Association and the occasional tug rate "wars" that occurred in Chicago during the late nineteenth century, but it is known that the Association advanced a tariff based upon the distance towed (considerable for the *Albrecht*) and the vessel's tonnage (minimal compared to the iron steamships beginning to populate the Great Lakes at that point).[69] If a somewhat arbitrary towage fee of $60 is included in the vessel's expenses, reflecting the need for tugs at both Chicago and Muskegon, the voyage's gross is further reduced to around $300. To also be factored in is a portion of the annual salary for Hackley & Hume's agent at Chicago, Deming, and the cost of provisions for the vessel, as well as miscellaneous fees and taxes, and, of course, the constant costs of maintaining the wooden vessel had to be amortized for the year.

Generally laying up for the winter at Chicago, the schooner underwent refurbishing there, typically at the Miller Brothers shipyard on the North Branch just above Chicago Avenue. Here the *Hume* received a new forecastle in 1883-1884 and the next year, at the Chicago Dry Dock Company yard, the recaulking of its hull, and even more caulking later that season at Miller Brothers.[70] The vessel's most significant maintenance work appears to have occurred in 1879 when, as the *H. C. Albrecht* and following its first year of service for Hackley & McGordon, the vessel went into dry dock at Muskegon to have new keelsons installed.[71] It is probable that at this point the vessel's rig was changed from two to three masts. Knowledge of this conversion is derived from a March 1937 *Chicago Tribune* article in which a former *Albrecht* crewman, William Drumm, recalled that the vessel had, at some undisclosed date, "a third-stick added." While it remains possible that the conversion took place in Chicago while William Walsh owned the vessel, it seems more likely it took place in Muskegon during the keelson replacement. Since the main and foremast were anchored in the main keelson and the masts' positions most likely readjusted to accommodate a third mast and accompanying sail, the replacement of the keelsons would have been a convenient point at which to restep the original masts. Although it seems counter-intuitive, adding a third mast was actually a cost-saving measure. The *Albrecht* when built was among the largest two-masted schooners on the Great Lakes. The addition of a third mast could actually reduce labor costs by reducing the number of seamen necessary to handle the large amount of canvas flying from those two masts. Three masts, each with smaller sails, yet providing a similar amount of canvas as two large sails, would be more manageable for a smaller crew. So, it appears that relatively soon after acquiring the *Albrecht*, Hackley & McGordon searched for ways to reduce further the vessel's operating costs, its apparent profit margin on its fleet continually decreasing as costs escalated and rates fell. Indeed, the only two-masted schooner constructed at Manitowoc larger than the *H. C. Albrecht*, the *Fleetwing* built three years earlier, would be converted to three masts five years later, in 1885.[72] In fact, enrollment records maintained by the Milwaukee Public Library show more than thirty, two-masted vessels similarly converted. Curiously, subsequent enrollments for the both the *Thomas Hume* and the *Fleetwing* did not make note of the rig change. Both vessels would eventually be lost as three-masted rigs although their final official documents still listed two masts.

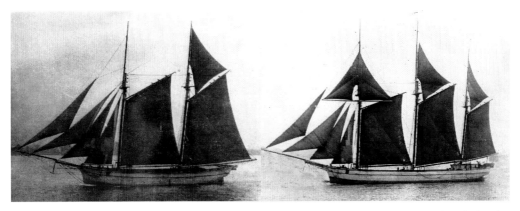

This comparison of the two-masted schooner Ontario *on the left to the three-masted schooner* Hattie Hutt *on the right shows how much smaller the sails are on the three-masted schooner, which would have been easier to handle and reduced the number of necessary crew. C. Patrick Labadie Collection, Alpena County Fletcher Library.*

The Decline of the Lumbering Industry

Although Hackley & McGordon exhibited good business sense initially in forming its fleet to carry its lumber to market, that example would be followed by a large number of lumber producers on both sides of Lake Michigan who would acquire their own vessels to transport their respective lumber. This rather rapidly diminished the firm's competitive advantage as a greater number of lumber firms began operating schooners and even steam craft in the Lake Michigan lumber trade. The emergence of fleets owned by lumber firms undercut the rates set by the Chicago Vessel Owners' Association, and made the lumber trade on Lake Michigan hardly as lucrative as it had been following the Great Fire.[73] Unsurprisingly, by the early 1880s, not long after purchasing the *H. C. Albrecht* from William Walsh, Hackley & Hume began looking to dispose of its fleet. The numbers were clear: In 1883, for example, Hackley & Hume's schooner *Rouse Simmons*, a slightly smaller vessel than the *Albrecht* built at Milwaukee in 1868, produced a profit of over $1600. If it is assumed the *Simmons* made about the same number of trips in 1883 as did the *Albrecht*, twenty-one, the average profit per voyage amounted to around $76, hardly a great sum.[74] The next year, as receding lumber freight rates took hold, the vessel realized a profit of less than a quarter of that of the previous year, averaging, assuming the *Simmons* sailed the equivalent of the *Hume*'s thirty trips, a mere $13.50 per voyage.[75] Because of declining profits on its schooner operations, by 1890 Hackley & Hume masters would realize only a third the salary they had enjoyed less than a decade

One of Hackley & McGordon's first vessels, and the last one to be sold, the Rouse Simmons *had the longest career with the company, later gaining fame as the Christmas Tree Ship lost in 1912 while carrying evergreens to Chicago for the holiday. Author's Collection.*

before.[76] Maintaining its relatively large schooner fleet in light of a receding market provoked Hackley & Hume to dispatch one of its vessel masters, Captain Charles Eggert, to Chicago in January 1884, who would be, in the words of Cleveland's *Marine Record*, "endeavoring to find purchasers for some of Hackley & Hume's vessels."[77] There were no takers. Aside from the decline in lumber rates brought about by the influx of craft into the Chicago lumber trade, and particularly those controlled by the lumber interests, another factor arose that brought about the schooners eventual demise. Both ship owners and lumber producers began to realize the value of steam propulsion for lumber carriers in the 1870s. These vessels could be built of wood along the general hull configuration of a schooner but with a deeper keel, since the major lumber ports on the east shore of Lake Michigan from Charlevoix to St. Joseph had, by the 1870s, relatively accessible and deep channels and harbors. The initial cost of the steamer with its power plant would certainly be more expensive than of a comparable schooner. In addition, some of its crew had to have the technical expertise to run the engines, boilers, and other related machinery. Clearly, too, the steam-powered vessel relied upon purchased fuel, initially wood slabs and later coal, an additional cost, rather than free wind. However, the ability of the steam-powered vessel to deliver relatively large amounts of lumber on a relatively consistent schedule, unconstrained by the vagaries of weather or wind as with a schooner, would prove the ultimate demise of the Great Lakes schooner early in the twentieth century. A convincing example is that of the steam barge *Albert Soper*, built 1881 at Grand Haven, Michigan, by Duncan Robertson for one of the consignees of Hackley & Hume lumber, the Soper & Pond Lumber Company of Chicago, established 1878 at Chicago.[78] Originally, the *Albert Soper* was a typical "rabbit" steamer, with pilothouse and all accommodations aft. During the winter of 1884-1885 at Chicago, its pilothouse was moved forward over the forecastle and nine feet cut off its aft cabin, allowing the vessel to carry 50,000 more board feet of lumber.[79] The *Albert Soper* measured 143 feet in length and twenty-eight feet in beam, just over ten feet in length and two feet in beam larger than the *Thomas Hume*, but in 1886 in forty-eight trips from east shore ports to Chicago that season carried an average of 396,000 board feet of pine.[80] By comparison, that season the *Thomas Hume* executed twenty-three trips averaging slightly more than 250,700 board feet, or half as many trips as the *Soper* carrying 156,000 less board feet per trip.[81] Clearly, the scales of economies afforded by steamers had begun to undercut the dominance of the schooner in the Lake Michigan lumber trade.

By the 1890s, the entire lumber trade at Chicago began to change. By the year 1882, three years following Hackley & McGordon's purchase of the *H. C. Albrecht*, the amount of lumber shipped to Chicago by water peaked, and began a steady decline as railroads carried increasingly more traffic.[82] However, it was not the railroads taking the Michigan white pine traffic, since the production of that wood also had declined as the existing stands of pine in the lower peninsula of Michigan disappeared. By 1894, certainly affected by the Panic of 1893, the Muskegon mills produced a little over 100 million board feet, a seventh of what had been produced a decade earlier.[83] Instead, the railroads began bringing to Chicago yellow pine from the south and Douglas fir and cedar from the west.[84] Faced with dwindling supplies of regional pine, Lake Michigan lumbermen began turning their attention away from the Midwest to fresh stands of timber to cut elsewhere in the country in order to remain in business. Hackley & Hume, being shrewd lumbermen and well aware of the rapidly receding supply of Michigan pine, began as early as 1886 investing in tracts of yellow pine in Louisiana, Mississippi, and Arkansas.[85] By the end of the century, the southern states would account for 32 percent of the timber produced in the nation, with the Great Lakes states providing 25 percent.[86] On November 17, 1894, the Hackley & Hume mill at Muskegon sawed its last pine log, and four years later the firm sold its last schooner, the *Rouse Simmons*, which had operated at a loss for several years.[87] The company would not need to find a buyer for the *Thomas Hume* because it went missing on May 21, 1891, the only vessel ever lost by Hackley & Hume, and its only fatal shipping accident. During its fourteen years utilized by Hackley & Hume, the *Thomas Hume* had an impressive career, making 409 round trips from Muskegon to Chicago and delivering about 94 million board feet of lumber, enough timber to construct about 31,000 average-sized residential homes.

1   Plumb, Ralph G., *A History of Manitowoc County* (Manitowoc: Brandt Printing and Binding Co.: 1904), 17, 19; *The History of Northern Wisconsin*, v. II (Chicago: Western Historical Publishing Co., 1881), 528.

2   *The History of Northern Wisconsin*, v. II, 527-528.

3   Tom Wenstadt, *The Freighters of Manitowoc: the Story of Great Lakes Freight Carrying Vessels Built in Manitowoc, Wisconsin* (Bloomington, Indiana: Authorhouse: 2007), 27-41; Manitowoc *Pilot*, February 15, 1867.

4   Louis Falge, *History of Manitowoc County, Wisconsin*, v. 2 (Chicago: Goodspeed Historical Association, 1912), 661-662.

5   Manitowoc *Pilot, ibid*.

6   Manitowoc *Pilot*, June 16, 1870.

7   Derived from Tom Wenstadt, *The Freighters of Manitowoc: The Story of Great Lakes Freight Carrying Vessels Built in Manitowoc*, 1-29.

8   *Manitowoc Pilot*, March 17, 1870; *Detroit Free Press*, December 21, 1867.

9   *Manitowoc Pilot*, March 17, 1870.

10 James Grant Wilson and John Fisk, eds., *Appletons's Cyclopædia of American Biography*, v. 2 (New York, D. Appleton & Co., 1888), 765-766.

11 John W. Ryckman, ed., *Report of the International Maritime Exhibition, Boston, 1889*-1890 (Boston: Hockwell & Churchill, 1890), 55-56.

12 Howard I. Chappelle, *The History of American Sailing Ships* (New York: W. W. Norton & Co., Inc., 1935), 221-223, 268-269; Theodore J. Karamanski, *Schooner Passage: Sailing Ships and the Lake Michigan* Frontier (Detroit: Wayne State University Press, 2000), 28-29.

13 Wenstadt, 5; Ryckman, 56.

14 James T. White, ed., *The National Cyclopædia of American Biography*, v. 1 (New York: Jas. T. White & Co., 1898), 502.

15 *Bold & Smithing's Manitowoc City Directory for 1880*, (Manitowoc: Bold & Smithing, 1880), 66; *Manitowoc Pilot*, July 14, 1870.

16 Mary Dopp, "Geographical Influences in the Development of Wisconsin. Chapter V. The Lumber Industry," *Bulletin of the American Geographical Society* (v. 45, no. 10) 1913: 738.

17 Information here and *in passim* relating to the construction of the typical Great Lakes schooner is derived from H. C. Inches, *The Great Lakes Wooden Shipbuilding Era* (Vermilion, Ohio: H. C. Inches, 1962); Loudon G. Wilson, "Great Lakes Sailing Craft of the Past Years: A Collection of Data, Facts, and Diagrams Covering Commercial Sail Vessels on the Inland Seas during the Period from their Inception to their Demise," unpublished mss., Historical Collections of the Great Lakes, Bowling Green State University; and W. J. Thompson, *Wooden Shipbuilding: A Comprehensive Manual for Wooden Shipbuilders to which is Added a Masting and Rigging Guide* (Chicago: A. C. McClurg & Co., 1918).

18 *Manitowoc Pilot*, 31 March 1870.

19 *Manitowoc Pilot*, 21 April 1870.

20 *Ibid.*

21 *Ibid.*, May 5, 1870.

22 *Ibid.*, June 16, 1870.

23 *Ibid.*

24 *Ibid.*, June 30, 1870; July 27, 1871; September 21, 1871; 30 May 1872. *Chicago Daily Tribune*, October 19, 1871.

25 Fred W. Kohlmeyer, "Lumber Distribution and Marketing in the United States," *Journal of Forest History* (April 1983): 87.

26 *Ibid.*

27 *Manitowoc Pilot*, September 25, 1873.

28 *Ibid*, October 17, 1891; *Marine Record*, November 4, 1897; *Der Nord-Westen*, April 5, 1906.

29 Permanent Enrollment No. 104, issued January 24, 1873; *Detroit Free Press*, December 6, 1873.

30 A. T. Andreas, *History of Chicago from the Earliest Period to the Present Time*, v. 2 (Chicago: A. T. Andreas Co, 1884).

31 *Chicago Daily Tribune*, April 7, 1874; June 5, 1875; September 11, 1875; November 17, 1875.

32 Andreas, *ibid.*

33 Wenstadt, 77; *Door County Advocate*, August 3, 1889.

34 Rolland H. Maybee, *Michigan's White Pine Era, 1840-1890* (Michigan History Division, Michigan Department of State: Lansing, 1973), 45, 52.

35 Richard Henry Harms, *Life after Lumbering: Charles Henry Hackley and the Emergence of Muskegon, Michigan* (Garland Publishing Co.: New York, 1989), 31-32.

36 *Ibid.*, 22, 51.

37 Harms, 100, 150. Harms states that the Chicago Vessel Owners' Association began fixing lumber freight rates at "non-competitive levels" in the 1870s, but that organization was not founded until 1881. See Harms, 76, and *Marquis' Handbook of Chicago: A Complete History, Reference Book and Guide to the City* (Chicago: A. N. Marquis & Co., 1887), 266.

38 Harms, 77; Andreas.

39 Maybee, 45.

40 J. B. Mansfield, *History of the Great Lakes*, v. 2 (Chicago: J. H. Beers & Co., 1899), 489-490.

41 *Marine Record*, May 26, 1883; June 9, 1883.

42 U. S. Patent 491472, February 7, 1893.

43 U. S. Patent 560747, May 26, 1896.

44 U. S. Patent 328559, October 20, 1885; *Marine Record*, October 15, 1885.

45 U. S. Patent 278847, June 5, 1883; *Marine Record*, May 23, 1883.

46 License of Enrolled Vessel, No. 61, Grand Haven, Michigan, August 23, 1890.

47 Harms, 116.

48 Margaret Ann Bank's recollections of her husband. Sherman Family Archives.

49 Contract between Thomas Hume, William Hume, and John Stevenson December 6, 1862. Lakeshore Museum Center Archives.

50 April 28, 1870, Letter from Stevenson and Aiken. Michigan State University Archives and Historical Collections, Hackley & Hume Papers, 1859-1955. 00097

51 Margaret Ann Bank's recollections of her husband. Sherman Family Archives.

2 Contract between Thomas Hume, William Hume and John Stevenson December 6, 1862. Lakeshore Museum Center Archives.

53 Enrollment document

54 *Ibid.*, 27.

55 Kohlmeyer, 87.

56 *Ibid.*

57 Derived from information in account books, Michigan State University Archives and Historical Collections, Hackley & Hume Papers, 1859-1955. 00097, hereafter cited as "account books." Hackley & Hume would operate another "Thomas Hume," as well, the name given to a steam engine the firm purchased in 1887 for use on its Clare County, Michigan, logging railroad, the Lake George & Muskegon River Railroad Company; see Harms, 121-127.

58 *Ibid.*

59 *Ibid, History of Muskegon County, Michigan, with Illustrations and Biographical Sketches of Some of Its Prominent Men and Pioneers* (Chicago: H. R. Page & Co., 1882), 25-28.

60 Harms, 148.

61 Derived from Hackley account books.

62 Harms, 155; Karamanski, 148; Luke Grant, "Industrial Democracy: The Longshoremen's Association," *The New Outlook* (v. 48, December 1, 1906),: 826-828.

63 *Twenty-Third Annual Report of the Commissioner of Labor, 1908: Workers' Insurance and Benefits Funds in the United States* (Washington, D. C.: Government Printing Office, 1909), 160-161.

64 Hackley account books.

65 Harms, 149.

66 *Chicago Tribune*, August 16, 1884.

67 *Ibid.*, April 30, 1883.

68 "The Chicago River and Harbor," *Railway Age* (v. 31, no. 2: January 11, 1901), 22; G. D. Urquhardt, *Dues and Shipping in Foreign Ports: A Manual of Reference for the Use of Shipowners, Shipbrokers, and Ship Masters* (London: George Philip and Son, Ltd.: 1908): 657.

69 See, for example, *Chicago Tribune*, April 9, 1884, and June 17, 1885.

70 *Marine Record*, May 1, 1884; May 28, 1885; October 15, 1885.

71 *Chicago Tribune*, April 29, 1880

72 Wenstadt, 23.

73 Harms, 148.

74 Hackley account books.

75 *Ibid.*

76 I*bid.*, 149.

77 *Marine Record*, January 3, 1884.

78 Albert Nelson Marquis, ed., *The Book of Chicagoans: A Biographical Dictionary of Living Leading Men of the City of Chicago* (Chicago: A. N. Marquis Co., 1911), 544.

79 *Marine Record*, January 1 , 1885.

80 *Ibid*, December 9, 1886.

81 Calculated from Hackley account books. The *Thomas Hume* began its season quite late that year because of a lumber shovers' strike at Chicago.

82 Kohlmeyer, 87.

83 Maybee, 45.

84 Kohlmeyer, 87.

85 Harms, 225-226.

86 Kohlmeyer, 88.

87 Harms, 142-143, 150.

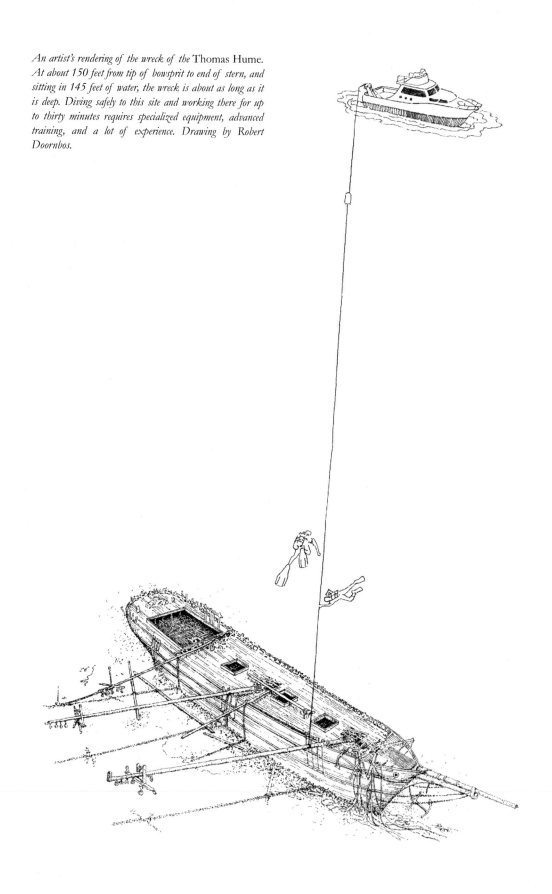

An artist's rendering of the wreck of the Thomas Hume. *At about 150 feet from tip of bowsprit to end of stern, and sitting in 145 feet of water, the wreck is about as long as it is deep. Diving safely to this site and working there for up to thirty minutes requires specialized equipment, advanced training, and a lot of experience. Drawing by Robert Doornbos.*

Planning the
INVESTIGATION

In the wake of the media announcement regarding the discovery of the *Thomas Hume*, Palmisano and Strunka continued to conduct research and visit the wreck over the next several summers, logging among themselves, Bud Brain, and Bob Schmidt, over one hundred dives. They never moved any artifacts from their original locations. Although they were not the only people to possess site coordinates, they did not publicize the location: They realized the vessel may be important enough to warrant an archaeological survey, and did not want other divers disturbing things. Considering the site is far from shore and deep, the time, cost, and skills needed to reach the wreck deterred all but a few hardy divers from making the trip. The team hoped that those divers who would make the effort would respect the integrity of the wreck. In the late summer of 2009, Palmisano contacted Michigan Shipwreck Research Associates (MSRA) to request its participation in conducting a more extensive survey of the shipwreck believed to be the *Thomas Hume*.

Michigan Shipwreck Research Associates

Established in 2001, MSRA is a Holland, Michigan-based non-profit organization, the mission of which is to foster wider public appreciation for Michigan's maritime history through research, exploration, documentation, and interpretation of its submerged maritime history. Although the wreck is in Illinois waters, the vessel's connection to Michigan's lumbering history makes it of great significance to Michigan, and MSRA's wide range of experience in the documentation of shipwrecks made it the obvious choice as a partner. Even before its formal incorporation in 2001, MSRA worked in cooperation with shipwreck explorer David Trotter as well as nationally acclaimed author Clive Cussler to search for and survey a number of significant historic vessels lost off west Michigan, finding fourteen vessels in as many years. These discoveries have prompted *in-situ* archaeological surveys, books, museum exhibits, documentary films, and public lectures. MSRA's work has been responsible for an increased awareness of Michigan's maritime history throughout western and southwestern Michigan, in particular, and in the Great Lakes region as well.

MSRA planned its first dive on the *Hume* in late summer 2009 as soon as weather allowed. After reviewing the coordinates, the team decided to launch its boat at New Buffalo, Michigan, the Michigan port nearest to the wreck, although still requiring a twenty-four-mile run to the site. The Chicago team had been launching from

South Chicago, Illinois, which required a similar run-time. When MSRA reached the site, the electronics on board switched to Illinois time, confirming what the team had plotted: The wreck lies about one-quarter mile into Illinois bottomlands.

Having already studied underwater video footage shot by the Chicago divers, MSRA divers had a good understanding of the wreck layout. On their initial dive, they followed the mooring line that the Chicago team had secured to the forward mast at a point just off the starboard side of the vessel. Natural light reached down to the lake bottom, and that visibility allowed them to see nearly the entire length of the wreck without the use of lights. After a perfunctory swim over the deck, one pair of divers entered the forward hatch and the other pair entered the aft hatch to explore below deck. Although natural light penetrated inside the wreck through the hatches and aft galley floor, they found that to see inside the forecastle, the forward-most space in the lower bow, they would need lights. Although they knew what to expect, the intact hull, empty lower cargo deck, and absence of silt reminded them how very significant the intact condition of this wreck is compared to other, more deteriorated wrecks. Most of the ship's gear and crew possessions remain inside the vessel just as they would have been at the time of the sinking, altered only by the sinking event and time underwater.

The *Thomas Hume* as a Time Capsule

When a vessel sinks, it suffers many changes until the remains eventually reach equilibrium with the new environment. Initially, the sinking process changes a vessel from an organized form to an unstable structure. Heavy items sink rapidly, lighter items may drift before sinking, while buoyant items may float away completely,

A section through the length of the wreck shows the artifact distribution. Tools, galleyware, and a small boat are contained in the cargo hold below the floor of the cabin near the stern where they must have fallen when the cabin broke off during the sinking. Personal effects belonging to the crew, including clothing, shoes, jewelry, and pocket change were found in the forecastle at the bow. The space between these two areas is empty, because the vessel was returning to Muskegon empty. Drawing by Robert Doornbos.

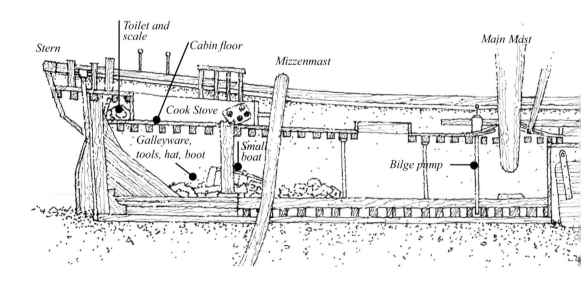

causing a filtering and scrambling of the material remains. The sudden arrival of the vessel on the lakebed can alter the natural movement of water currents, often resulting in new scour patterns in the surrounding sand. Once underwater, chemical processes and the action of biological organisms begin to disintegrate both organic and inorganic items, although at a much slower rate in the Great Lakes freshwater environment than in saltwater. Fabrics like the sails, clothing, and rope deteriorate first. However, wood that would decay completely in saltwater over just a few decades can last for centuries in freshwater. With care and detailed study, archaeologists can obtain information and draw conclusions from even the most scattered and deteriorated sites. Nevertheless, the archaeological information can be gathered more quickly and with better accuracy when a vessel is as intact as the *Hume*.

In the case of the *Hume*, the most catastrophic destruction took place during the sinking, when the trauma of the event forced the aft cabin off the vessel and when the masts fell off their steps. Certainly, some items on deck or inside the cabin must have been carried away in the sinking, but others settled down beneath the cabin floor in the cargo hold near the stern. A number of recognizable objects that would have been in the cabin lie scattered, and in some instances broken, in the lower hold. All around them lie short loose planks; some appear to have tongue-and-groove edges and may have once been cabin floor or wall planks. Except for one white pitcher found in the cargo hold on the port side near the middle of the vessel, there are no artifacts in the middle of the cargo hold. In the forecastle, the area below deck in the bow that served as sleeping quarters for the crew, there are myriad items of a more personal nature than those below the cabin floor. The complete separation of artifacts in the bow and stern adds to the site's overall interpretive value because there is little doubt about where the objects were located before the sinking. If studied, they could provide insight into life on board a nineteenth-century lumber schooner, a topic for which little information exists.

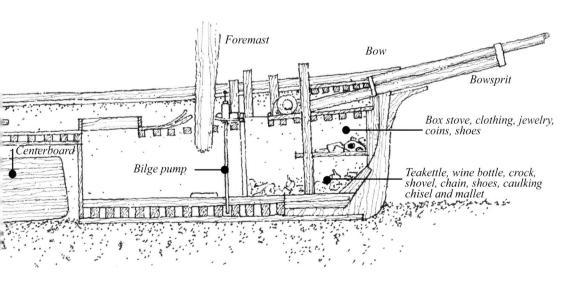

Early Diver-led Shipwreck Surveys

Most archaeologists in the Great Lakes region recognize that shipwrecks are invaluable historical resources, but they also realize they are recreational attractions for sport divers. Limited work force and budgets make the management and documentation of shipwrecks by state archaeologists a very low priority, and consequently officials have some concerns about the impact of diver traffic. In an article entitled *"Shipwreck Preservation in Michigan: Two Decades On,"* John Halsey, Michigan's recently retired state archaeologist, noted, "Sport divers—who are the underwater archeologist's main source for information and field crews—are also those chiefly responsible for disturbing these vessels."[1] He undoubtedly attributed this both to divers who alter the site on purpose when they collect souvenirs or move things around for a better photo opportunity, or indirectly by such things as throwing anchors or hooks that can damage the wrecks. In the article he also recognized that "To make a discovery is the dream of most sports divers. A virgin wreck is a high-class trophy. It is also the first and last chance to record the scene in a pristine state." While this may be true, it has been divers, not archaeologists, who have spearheaded some of the earliest underwater investigations of newly discovered shipwrecks in the Great Lakes.

The earliest diver-led project of great significance involved the previously mentioned raising of the 105-foot, two-masted schooner *Alvin Clark* in 1969 after 105 years underwater. Running light like the *Thomas Hume* when it sank, the *Clark* transported lumber, among other things, during its career. James Quinn, director of the Neville Public Museum in Green Bay, Wisconsin, cataloged artifacts recovered before and after divers raised the shipwreck. Some of the items included the captain's writing desk, a brass locket, a wallet, clay pipes, a water pitcher, a clock, an oil lamp, tools, and three pennies. Even a crock of cheese—still full—was pulled from the ship. Although the vessel deteriorated over twenty-five years out of water due to lack of funding for expensive concervation work, many artifacts survived. The Detroit Historical Society holds in its collection about 100 artifacts from the wreck.

Recreational divers also led an extensive survey on the 194-foot schooner *Lucerne*. For nearly a century, the circumstances surrounding the thirteen-year-old *Lucerne's* disappearance in 1886 remained a mystery, like that of the *Hume*. This changed when a group of avocational archaeologists, led by LaMonte Florentz, first located the wreck in shallow water in Lake Superior near Chequamegon Bay in the 1970s. They dredged sand out of the wreck and removed a number of artifacts during a 1977 investigation, many of which are presently on display at the Lake Superior Marine Museum in Duluth, Minnesota. Among more than 200 artifacts recovered are an overcoat, three felt hats, two vests, suspenders, socks, shoes, a rubber slicker, a woolen cap, kaolinite pipes, a pocketknife, bottles, a liquor flask, a glass oil chimney, a large syringe, sewing needles, and numerous other personal items. Additional excavations from the stern produced brass binoculars, an inkwell, calipers, a Grand Army of the Republic Civil War medal, boots, a leather Bible cover, and a brass alarm clock. Although Florentz created an inventory of the recovered items, he died in a car accident before he was able to interpret the materials.[2]

Since these two early surveys, numerous divers, individually or in groups, have discovered, surveyed, and videotaped a large number of shipwrecks, sharing their findings with other divers and the public largely through professional conferences and shipwreck film festivals. However, some resource managers consider surveys without historical interpretation and subsequent publications insufficient for the historical record. John Halsey observed, "Divers may take copious photographs and videos, and even make some drawings, but do little in the way of plotting individual remains. Once the wreck is opened [to divers], artifacts, if they do not disappear, are quickly displaced from where they were when the vessel came to rest. Research is focused on the wreck incident, seldom on the role of the vessel or the site in its archeological or historical context."[3] Although there have been some surveys conducted by recreational divers that do involve historical interpretation and result in publications, divers often tire of the laborious research, and instead move on to the next project. In this way, information that they might have gathered from the shipwreck is lost. However, there exist few funding sources to cover the expenses of professional archaeology and not every shipwreck is a candidate for full-scale archaeology unless the study of its remains offers the potential for new information.

In the years since the establishment of the Abandoned Shipwreck Act, which made shipwreck artifact recovery without a permit illegal, a large number of sport divers have developed a greater interest in archaeology than in the preceding years when diver interest may have been more focused on collecting artifacts. Several organizations made up of divers and historians have cropped up in the wake of the Abandoned Shipwreck Act, of which Michigan Shipwreck Research Associates is an example. Other groups such as the Underwater Archaeological Society of Chicago, Cleveland Underwater Explorers, the Maritime Archaeological Survey Team, the Great Lakes Shipwreck Research Foundation, the Great Lakes Shipwreck Historical Society, the Wisconsin Underwater Archaeological Society, the Great Lakes Shipwreck Preservation Society, and Save Ontario's Shipwrecks, among others, share similar missions to document, preserve, and interpret Great Lakes shipwrecks. These organizations have overseen survey efforts on a large number of shipwrecks. The results have varied from simply taking video to share with other divers, to near-professional level archaeology and publications. Archaeologists have seen the value of this new breed of diver/researcher and have often collaborated with them on several projects. David Cooper, Phillip Wright, Keith Mervedin, Frank Canteles, Tamara Thompson, Carrie Sowden, Kenneth Pott, Jeff Gray, Russ Green, and Paul Johnston, among other archaeologists, have led a number of surveys with the help of volunteer divers trained in archaeological techniques. These surveys have resulted in the documentation of collections of shipwrecks in such areas as Pictured Rocks, Apostle Islands, Thunder Bay, Manitou Passage, Lake Erie, and Wisconsin waters of Lake Michigan and Lake Superior. In fact, in 1990, a team of divers led by archaeologist David Cooper returned to the *Lucerne* for an in-depth survey of the wreck to complete the work of LaMonte Florentz after his passing. Collectively these surveys have added significant new data to the historic record. In addition, many of these projects have resulted in the listing of shipwrecks on the National Register of Historic Places.

Professional Archaeology in the Great Lakes

Archaeology usually involves three phases. Phase I investigation consists of a combination of background research and fieldwork designed to identify resources and define site boundaries. Phase II investigation is conducted in order to test or evaluate an archaeological site's eligibility for inclusion in the National Register of Historic Places. Phase III investigation involves artifact recovery, conservation, and interpretation. Professional archaeological work on shipwrecks involving Phase III artifact recovery has been very limited in the Great Lakes. Three projects are worth mentioning because of the significant amount of data gathered. The 1858-built propeller *Indiana* was lost in 1858 in Lake Superior off Crisp Point, Michigan. The site was discovered in 1972 and declared eligible for the National Register of Historic Places in 1978. Beginning in 1979, and for several years thereafter, the Smithsonian Institution's National Museum of American History, recovered propulsion and other machinery from the *Indiana*, documenting various aspects of the wreck site as well. From 1991 to 1993, the museum undertook further archaeological investigations. At the time of this book's printing, an exhibit is on display at the National Museum of American History that features data and artifacts from the *Indiana*.

Between 1985 and 1991, archaeologist Kenneth Pott, then with the Michigan Maritime Museum in South Haven, Michigan, led a project to document the newly discovered two-masted scow *Rockaway*. Used to haul lumber during the later years of its career, the *Rockaway* sank in 1891, the same year that the *Hume* disappeared. A fisherman found it by accident when his nets became entangled in 1985. Although a shallow-water, scattered site, the *Rockaway* revealed dozens of artifacts on the wreck or buried in sand. Personal possessions included shoes and work boots (all lefts), two smoking pipe bowls, a partial but otherwise intact section of a cotton vest, a two-bladed jackknife with antler body with silver embellishment, and an engraved gold face to a pocket watch. In an extensive excavation, Pott and his team recovered these artifacts and dozens more and conserved them for display. Although no longer on display, the artifacts are held by the Michigan State Museum and can be seen by appointment.

Soon after a boy discovered in 1990 the bow of a wooden ship projecting from the eroding west bank of the Millecoquins River in Naubinway, Michigan, state archaeologist John Halsey, with the support of the Association for Great Lakes Maritime History, conducted a professional examination of the vessel. The Association for Great Lakes Maritime History raised funds to bring in a student team from East Carolina University to conduct an archaeological excavation at the site and recover, curate, and display artifacts from the vessel. The team recovered hand-wrought hooks and rigging thimbles, rough hewn timbers and pre-Civil War bottle forms, and china styles all typical of the early years of Michigan statehood. Twenty-eight barrels were excavated in 1994, a few still containing well-preserved fish remains. Remarkably, archaeologists found legible paper shipping labels when they excavated a box of tea. Although they could not positively identify the schooner, archaeologists confirmed it dated back to the 1830s or 40s, and was probably involved in the commercial fishing trade. University professors Dr. Bradley Rogers and Frank Cantelas noted that the artifacts recovered from the Millecoquins site make it the most important shipwreck on the Great Lakes for understanding how people lived, traded, and built small sailing craft in the early nineteenth century.[4]

Planning the Archaeological Investigation of the *Thomas Hume*

Based upon the survey work conducted by the Chicago team on the *Thomas Hume*, the equivalent of Phase I archaeological survey, and MSRA's subsequent historic research and site evaluation, MSRA realized that the wreck may be eligible for the National Register of Historic Places. Criteria for eligibility includee,

1.Sites that are associated with events that have made a significant contribution to the broad patterns of our history; or,

2.Sites that are associated with the lives of persons significant in our past; or,

3.Sites that embody distinctive characteristics of a type, period, or method of construction, or that represent the work of a master, or that possess high artistic values, or that represent a significant and distinguishable entity whose components may lack individual distinction; or,

4.Sites that have yielded, or may be likely to yield, information important in prehistory or history.

The wreck of the *Hume* is intact, has a connection to lumber barons Charles Hackley and Thomas Hume; represents the work of a master schooner builder from Manitowoc, Wisconsin; has distinction of being the first wire-rigged schooner built in Manitowoc; and contains a wealth of cultural materials that could yield significant new information about life aboard a nineteenth-century lumber schooner.

For two significant reasons, MSRA turned to the Lakeshore Museum Center in Muskegon, Michigan, to propose collaborating on an archaeological investigation. First, the museum owns and operates the Hackley and Hume historic home museums, the residences of the *Thomas Hume* owners, making it a very appropriate institution with which to partner. Second, two members of the museum staff, executive director John McGarry and collections manager Dani LaFleur, are both divers and have extensive experience in underwater archaeology. McGarry served as executive director for the Mel Fisher Maritime Heritage Society in Key West, Florida, holding primary responsibility for the development and organization of a research and exhibit facility for artifacts associated with shipwreck *Atocha*, a Spanish treasure vessel found by adventurer Mel Fisher. LaFleur served as a graduate assistant at East Carolina University's conservation lab conducting artifact conservation and database preparation on *Queen Anne's Revenge*, pirate Blackbeard's vessel. The Lakeshore Museum Center showed great interest in establishing a joint venture partnership to study and interpret for the public the *Thomas Hume* and possibly host a related museum exhibit. The *Hume* played a significant role in transporting vast quantities of Muskegon County lumber to Chicago during the last quarter of the nineteenth century, and there would be no better facility to present that history than the Lakeshore Museum Center whose mission is to preserve and interpret the natural and cultural history of Muskegon County.

With the proceeds from their thriving lumber business Charles Hackley and Thomas Hume had side-by-side Victorian mansions built on Webster Avenue in Muskegon, Michigan, in 1887. As the senior partner, Hackley's more ornate home on the left reflects his stature in the company. The homes shared a carriage house between them. Lakeshore Museum Center Collection.

Officials at the Lakeshore Museum Center agreed that the wreck of the *Hume* had the potential to offer new insights into the transportation of lumber and life aboard a nineteenth-century schooner, about which little is known. Very few historical documents remain to depict this aspect of the lumbering industry and, consequently, archaeologists and historians have to rely on the examples that remain on the bottom of the lakes for information, and build upon information already gathered from other shipwrecks. Unfortunately, although stories abound of schooners found loaded with artifacts in the early days of sport diving, many succumbed to diver pilfering and little remains except vague memories. A number of organizations have conducted Phase I and II surveys on newly discovered "virgin" schooners throughout the Great Lakes, but little cultural material was found or documented on these shipwrecks, and few reports are available for review and comparison. Only the *Alvin Clark, Lucerne,* and *Rockaway* mentioned previously, each of which contained a wealth of cultural material recorded in publications, can serve as comparison for the artifacts found on the *Thomas Hume*. Fortunately, these vessels share some similarities in type, size, and vintage to the *Thomas Hume*.

To fund the development of a research plan to determine the feasibility of a survey on the *Thomas Hume*, MSRA turned to the Michigan Humanities Council to make application for a planning grant, which it received in 2009. LMC and MSRA developed a plan for an archaeological survey, a museum exhibit, a curriculum guide, a documentary film, and a public event. The team then applied for and received a major matching grant from the Michigan Humanities Council. Although the project duration would be eighteen months, the grant schedule would only encompass one summer for fieldwork on the wreck. Considering the schedule and the need to document the vessel before divers began regularly visiting the site, the team would need to compress the documentation process. MSRA and the LSM would begin the process in Phase II, which typically ends with a formal nomination of the site to the National Register. However, because the MHC does not fund National Register nominations, the team would have to delay that until after Phase III, in which they would conduct more detailed data recovery. Although Phase III often involves full artifact recovery and conservation, the team would need a permit from the State of Illinois, along with additional funding for that portion of the work. Artifact preservation is one of the most important considerations when planning or implementing any action that will result in the recovery of material from a marine archaeological site. Organic and inorganic materials taken out of a wet environment and exposed to air decay at a fast pace unless stabilized. It is the responsibility of the excavator to see that material recovered is properly conserved and will have a home in perpetuity. The conservation phase is time-consuming and expensive, often costing more than the original excavation. Without conservation, however, most artifacts will perish, and important historic data will be lost to those who may wish to reexamine the material in the future.

In order to limit costs, and leave many artifacts for future divers to observe in their environment on the wreck, the team considered the possibility of selecting only a few artifacts for recovery, conservation, and museum display. In reviewing footage and still images of artifacts on the wreck, the team identified a small number of items that would be relatively easy and economical to conserve, would yield more data through their study than could be extracted underwater, and would offer significant interpretive value in a museum exhibit. And, the team received a private grant to cover the work. However, obtaining the permit could prove difficult considering that throughout the Great Lakes, only a few permits have been issued for the recovery of artifacts from a shipwreck since the establishment of the Abandoned Shipwreck Act. Hesitation in issuing these permits may stem from budget cuts leaving state employees overworked, pressure from divers to leave artifacts in place for their viewing pleasure, or bitterness after a handful of legal cases in which individuals have sued for shipwreck ownership rights and won.

Having past experience with Illinois for permitted recovery of the artifacts from the *Wells Burt*, co-author van Heest contacted the Illinois Historic Preservation Agency (IHPA) to discuss recovering, conserving, and displaying a small number of select artifacts within the context of a traveling exhibit. With funding in place for conservation, professional archeologists to oversee the work, and a venue for public display, the team had everything necessary to properly recover and analyze the artifacts, except a permit. IHPA Deputy State Historic Preservation Officer Ann Hacker reviewed the project plans and gave a tentative approval for limited artifact recovery pending review of a detailed project proposal by Illinois State Archaeologist Joe Phillippe. After his review, Phillippe informed MSRA that although no permit would be needed to dive or survey the wreck, he would *not* issue a permit for the recovery of artifacts. He gave no reason for the denial except to indicate that the artifacts should be "left where they are to best preserve their integrity for future study." Considering that MSRA and LSM would be conducting a professional survey 120 years after the sinking, it seemed the "future" had already arrived. However, valuable archaeological information could not be obtained without recovering the artifacts. And the public would lose out on the opportunity to see the artifacts in person. In addition, sport diver traffic to the site would be increasing, and although most divers respect the law, it is unrealistic to assume the best from everyone. Artifacts will undoubtedly be handled, moved, and possibly pilfered. The *Hume* would not remain pristine for any other future archaeological studies. The response from the IHPA seemed rather shortsighted.

Not wishing to pursue a legal alternative, LMC and MSRA opted to proceed with all aspects of the project without artifact recovery. However, in order to learn anything of value from the artifacts, divers would need to make more dives and spend longer time on the bottom, adding cost to the project and risk to the divers. Unfortunately, even with these adjustments, archaeologists could not expect to learn as much from an artifact without the ability to study it in a laboratory setting. MSRA obtained supplemental grants from the Great Lakes Shipwreck Research Foundation, the Great Lakes Cruising Club and the Gertz Foundation to cover additional project expenses and the dive team members made personal commitments for increased participation. McGarry, LaFleur, and Valerie van Heest began developing research objectives, realizing the team would be attempting one of the most comprehensive *in-situ* surveys yet conducted in the Great Lakes.

---

1 John Halsey, "Shipwreck Preservation in Michigan: Two Decades On," *Contested Waters* Fall/Winter 1996, vol. 1 (3/4)

2 David Cooper, *Fire, Ice and Storm* (Wisconsin: State Historical Society of Wisconsin, 1991)

3 Ibid.

4 http://www.hal.state.mi.us/mhc/museum/explore/museums/hismus/special/schooner/questions.html.

Archaeological divers use acrylic slate boards and plasticized paper called Mylar to record dimensions and data. A regular lead pencil works underwater.

CHAPTER
FIVE

Archaeological
FIELD WORK

The Lakeshore Museum Center and Michigan Shipwreck Research Associates formed three broad research goals for the fieldwork: To confirm the identity of the shipwreck, to extract information about shipboard life on a lumber schooner, and to develop an understanding of the circumstances of the sinking, which has long been considered mysterious. While many archaeological projects strive to record hull structure and ship's equipment, the tight schedule for this project required the team to limit the study to features that could provide identification clues and help explain the sinking, and those unique to the shipment of lumber and the shipboard life of the crew. Since the hull retains its integrity and will likely remain unchanged in the near future, additional survey work, if deemed necessary, can be conducted by this team or other teams. Project fieldwork objectives included videotaping and capturing still images of the wreck for interpretation and exhibit work, producing a scaled site plan, developing a video mosaic image of the wreck, recording the general position of the artifacts, developing an artifact inventory, and, if time allowed, gathering specific details about each artifact. In addition, the team hoped to locate evidence to determine whether the vessel carried passengers on its last trip, as suggested by the note found in the bottle a few months after the disappearance.

Fieldwork operations were limited to the summer of 2010, a brief period, made even briefer by the large number of days in which winds made lake conditions too rough for work. Survey work began in June and lasted through early November. Visibility on site ranged from thirty feet to as much as one hundred feet. Rough waves often resulted in worse conditions in the days following. However, spring's cold water, which usually offers the highest visibility, instead provided cloudy water. July and August provided the best visibility. The gale force winds of late October stirred up the water, making visibility poor during the last few dives of the season.

Jack van Heest provided transportation to and from the site for the MSRA team with his 24-foot Bayliner. Although small, the boat could easily be towed south to the launch ramp in New Buffalo, Michigan, and is fuel-efficient. The vessel had adequate space to accommodate a maximum of five divers using double tanks. Tom Palmisano utilized his 23-foot Almar Sounder to transport the Chicago team to the wreck site. Prior to dive operations each day, the team held a dockside meeting to review safety gear, and discuss daily objectives, dive rotations, and any additional issues including weather, equipment, and safety concerns. The project director maintained daily logs recording time leaving dock, time on site, activities, general observations, and work accomplished.

Dive team members included Palmisano, Strunka, and Brain from Chicago and Jack van Heest, Craig Rich, Jeff Vos, Bob and Jan Underhill, Todd White, Tim Marr and Valerie van Heest (project director) from MSRA, all experienced technical divers capable of working safely at depth. McGarry and LaFleur provided archaeological direction, although they did not dive. Bottom times ranged from fifteen to fifty minutes with decompression as long as ninety minutes. Most divers wore dry suits for warmth. Some divers chose to limit bottom times and used only a single tank. However, most divers used double tanks and breathed mixed gas to allow for a clearer head at depth. Most carried nitrox in a second or third tank to breath during decompression and as emergency gas for the ascent. Some carried a fourth tank filled with oxygen to use in shallow depths to help shorten decompression times. Still others carried a small bottle of argon, a "warmer" gas to fill their dry suits, which allowed them to maintain more body heat during the long decompression. Each diver only made one dive per day.

The project director selected tasks and teamed up divers based on individual talents and skills. The buddy system of diving in pairs was adhered to for safety. Jack van Heest, Todd White, Jeff Vos, and Jeff Strunka served as team videographers. Jeff Vos, Jeff Strunka, Jack van Heest, Craig Rich, and Tim Marr took measurements using a 200-foot plastic construction tape measure. Robert and Jan Underhill shot natural light still photographs of the wreck with Nikonos III and Nikonos V film cameras. Vos and the other divers shot still images of the artifacts, using a compact digital Canon camera housing provided at wholesale cost from Ikelight specifically for the project. Palmisano often removed zebra mussels with a soft brush in preparation for observations and photography. He and Brain made detailed observations of ship structures from which the team could draw conclusions. Vos, the van Heests, Rich, and Strunka made detailed sketches of the individual artifacts. Divers recorded notes using regular lead pencils on a Mylar film affixed to custom-made acrylic slate boards.

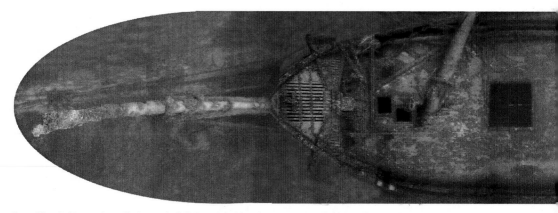

Created by stitching together video images by Jeff Strunka, this video mosaic image helps provide an understanding of the wreck site. Note the intact bowsprit, the fallen fore and main masts, the broken mizzenmast, and the missing cabin. Graphic by Valerie van Heest.

Team members (from left to right clockwise) Todd White, Bud Brain, Valerie van Heest, Jack van Heest, Jan Underhill, Tim Marr, Tom Palmisano, Bob Underhill, Jeff Strunka, Craig Rich, and Jeff Vos. Octogenarian Bud Brain served as an active member of the dive team. In 1969, he was a lead member of a team that raised the Alvin Clark, *a two-masted schooner that sank in Green Bay in 1864. Photograph by Rene Mireles.*

Hull and Deck Documentation

Early fieldwork included taking measurements of the vessel and major features on the deck as well as in the starboard debris field so that the project artist, Robert Doornbos, could create both two-dimensional and three-dimensional sketches. Once they completed that task, divers filmed the wreck in preparation for the creation of a video mosaic that would later be stitched together on computer. The intact condition of the vessel allowed this work to be completed in very few dives with significant ease. Review of the video and completion of the mosaic confirmed observations made while

diving: There is no damage of any kind to suggest a collision, a theory long held by mariners at the time of the *Hume*'s disappearance.

The team verified the measurements taken by the Chicago team in 2004 using plastic tape measures. At 136 feet from bow to stern, the wreck measured only slightly larger than the *Hume*'s enrolled length of 131.48 feet, but according to the Navigation Laws of the United States 1882 edition enrolled lengths were taken "from the fore part of the main stem to the after part of the stern post above the main deck,"[1] which would be several feet short of the overall length. The breadth was measured "at the broadest part about the main wales and the depth from the underside of the deck plank to the ceiling of the hold."[2] Measurements from these points, with some room for error, are 131 feet long, 26 feet breath, and 8 foot 6 inches deep. These measurements are compellingly close to the *Thomas Hume*'s enrolled dimensions of 131.6 feet long, 26.3 feet breadth, and 8.4 feet deep, substantiating its identity as the *Hume*.

Certain vessel features warrant some discussion beyond the initial observations made during early dives. The *Hume* appears to have been built with what could be

considered a half clipper bow first seen in schooners built in the 1850s by William Bates in Manitowoc, Wisconsin. The *Thomas Hume* features an attractive slanting knee that supports the bowsprit to give it the look of a clipper schooner. Its builder, Jasper Hanson, was most certainly influenced by this design pioneered by William Bates, father of the "Clipper Schooner," a design prevalent in Manitowoc in the 1860s and 70s near the time of the *H. C. Albrecht*'s build.

The wood stock starboard anchor remains attached to the wreck. The pile of chain that surrounds it, likely spilled from the deck when the vessel capsized. Video capture by Jack van Heest

The two different anchors on the shipwreck speak of its age when lost because the steel stock anchor is of newer vintage. The British adopted the steel stock anchors in the 1840s and the Americans in the 1880s, so the newer anchor was likely installed at least a decade after the vessel's building. The wooden stock anchor may have been original and, although old, would have still been useful. In fact, the wood stocks had an advantage because their buoyancy causes the anchor to fall crown first and would help the flukes dig in.[3]

The relative small size of the cargo hatches gave reason to ponder how longer boards of lumber could be loaded, particularly when the angle available became smaller as the hold filled higher. Some lumber schooners had built into the sides of the hull ports for loading lumber. However, divers found no such ports on the *Hume*. It must be concluded that the smaller hatches would minimize the potential intake of lake water, increase the deck space for supplemental cargo, and would not have posed any significant difficulty to the people responsible for loading lumber. In fact, it is a testament to the skill of shore-based skilled laborers, known as dock wallopers, to load a vessel efficiently.

Two fairleads exist on the stern rail but no wooden davits for securing a yawl boat are apparent at the stern as was common on schooners. It remains a possibility that the

Dock wallopers used stocking techniques to fill the schooner to full capacity inside the hold as this image of the replica schooner Challenge *at Discovery World in Milwaukee indicates. Photograph by Chris Winters.*

Hume had iron davits, which appeared on the Lakes about 1870 and were installed on the rail. However, zebra mussels obscure the place where they might have been secured. Additional documentation will need to be done to confirm this. If davits did exist, then they were completely ripped off in the sinking. If they did not exist, then the lifeboat, if Hackley's statement about the *Hume* having one is to be believed, may have been stowed upside down on the roof of the cabin.

Looking at the starboard hull of the wreck at deck level, the continuous gap for deck water runoff is visible. Video capture by Jack van Heest.

Vertical posts exist around the raised sterncastle deck. Rope would have passed through eyes in each one as protection for crew working on the deck. Video capture by Jack van Heest.

The bulwarks, which are the rails enclosing the deck, are solid from deck to rail except for a narrow and semi-continuous gap at the level of the deck for the drainage of water. This type of water discharge is seen on a number of schooners and seems efficient to deal with both rainwater and cresting waves, although as with any forms of scuppers, if they can let water out, they can also let water it in. Several schooners, including most of the vessels owned by Hackley & Hume had a raised rail, called a taff rail or monkey rail, around the sterncastle deck that surrounded the cabin. Instead, the *Hume* had a rope rail, confirmed by the presence of four vertical posts on the rails flanking each side of the cabin. Rope would have passed through these posts to provide some security for those working on the sterncastle deck. This feature will help to differentiate the *Hume* from many other schooners and gives rise to the possibility that the schooner pictured on page 38 and 54 in front of the Hackley & Hume lumber mill, sometime after 1881, is the *Hume*. That vessel does not have the more common raised taff rail.

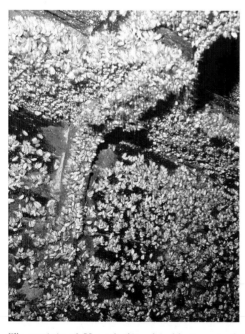

The proximity of Hanson's shipyard in Manitowoc to the Richards Foundry makes it likely that Hanson contracted with Richards for the Albrect's iron knees, an uncommon feature of schooners of the period. Photograph by Robert Underhill.

As would be expected of a lumber hauling vessel, there is little deck equipment, leaving the deck open for stacking lumber for larger shipments, a common practice. Only the bilge pump and centerboard winch (if one existed) would have taken up space aft of the windlass and forward of the cabin. There does not appear to be any evidence of sheet posts, a wooden horse for securing the mast booms. Perhaps, if they did exist at the time of the vessel's construction, they might have been eliminated when converted to three masts to leave more space for deck cargo. There does not appear to be any damage to the deck, suggesting they might have been forced off during the sinking.

The presence of ninety-degree hanging knees—brackets supporting the upper deck—offers evidence of the vessel's use for hauling lumber. Rounded wooden knees made from the crotch of a tree branch are more commonly seen on vessels of this period. They offered strength, but took up valuable cargo space. In fact, based on evidence on another shipwreck, it is known that the *Rouse Simmons*, one of Hackley & McGordon's other three-masted schooners, had traditional curved wooden knees.[4] Iron knees were more expensive than wood at first. They start appearing around the 1860s, introduced mainly by the Canadians who began working in iron before the Americans. Such a design feature may have made the vessel particularly attractive to Hackley and his partner McGordon when they purchased the *Hume*. The iron knees on the *Hume* may contribute to the good condition of the vessel after 120 years underwater.

As intact as is the *Thomas Hume,* unfortunately the cabin is missing, evidently forced off during the sinking. Cabins remain on only a few schooner wrecks such as the *F. T. Barney, Cornelia B. Windiate,* and *Marion Egan,* recently discovered in Lake Huron by David Trotter. When divers raised the *Alvin Clark,* its cabin was intact; however, unlike the *Hume,* the *Clark's* cabin ran the full width of the vessel, about twenty-five feet. A study of a scale model made of the *Clark's* cabin, in the collection of the Detroit Historical Society, can offer some ideas about how the *Hume's* cabin may have been configured. At only about eighteen feet wide, it is possible the *Hume's* cabin had a similar layout, although rather than double-stacked bunks, like the *Clark,* the sleeping space on the *Hume* appears to have been located at the cabin's floor level under the deck, a common layout for smaller cabins, and similar to the *Cornelia B. Windiate.* The distance from front to back of the cabin is enough to accommodate two people lengthwise with some additional space. It is likely that the captain's room was located in the starboard forward corner of the cabin, a feature found on the plans of several schooners. The first mate's room may have been just behind the captain's. The other side may have contained space for the galley and steward's room and a set of steps leading from the cabin to the stern deck.

One of the most perplexing artifacts in the cabin area is a piece of what appears to be heavy yellowish paper affixed to the wall at the head of the forwardmost bunk on the starboard side, assumed to be the captain's room. Four screws in the corners hold remnants of what may have been a glass covering and there exist shards of glass sitting on the wooden surface of the bunk below. There remains the possibility that it could have been a paper-backed mirror, although there was no trace of silver on the glass shards. Unfortunately, it can never be determined with certainty what hung on that cabin wall.

Divers found an interesting artifact in the lazaret, the storage space behind the aft wall of the cabin and just under the sterncastle deck. Crewmembers could access the lazeret

In what may have been the captain's cabin, often the forwardmost room on the starboard side, divers found the paper remnants of something approximately 16" by 30" mounted on the wall above the berth and broken glass below it. Photograph by Jeff Vos.

through a pair of small doors in the back wall of the cabin, assuming the layout is similar to what was recorded on the *Alvin Clark*. Since the cabin and any doors would have been swept away in the sinking, the space is now easily accessible. Swimming in, the divers discovered a large object covered by zebra mussels. Based on its shape, they realized it is a toilet. Toilets on vessels are called "heads" for one reason. Originally, crewmembers sat on boards with holes cut in them hanging over the sides of the ships. They were placed at the "head," or bow of the ship where a tailwind would carry the smells away from a vessel. The first patents for flushing water closets were issued in Scotland and England beginning in the 1770s. During that time, the majority of Americans were still using chamber pots or outhouses. Beginning in the mid 1870s, American inventors began patenting plunger-type water closets. However, the flush toilet did not gain popularity in the United States until after World War I, when American troops came home from England discussing the popularity of toilets there.[5] A toilet would have certainly been a luxury for a schooner crew in the 1880s or 1890s. Although not mounted when found in the lazaret, the position of the toilet on the starboard side of the wreck, just behind where the cabin once stood, suggests it may have been installed in the back corner of the cabin on the starboard side. It likely tumbled off its mount when the cabin broke off the vessel. Unfortunately, time did not allow divers to clean the mussels off the toilet to check for manufacturer's marks or a date, or search for a possible discharge port. Considering that neither the *Clark,* a much older vessel than the *Hume,* nor the more contemporary *Rockaway or Lucerne* had toilets at the time they sank, it seems unlikely that the *Hume,* when built as the *Albrecht,* had a toilet installed in 1870. More likely, the toilet was added to the *Hume* at some point late in its career as toilets became more common on vessels, perhaps at the time of its conversion to a three-masted schooner when the cabin would have been adjusted to accommodate the mizzenmast. The *Grampian,* built just three years after the *Hume* sank, had a toilet in its cabin. By then, it had become more common to see these conveniences aboard commercial vessels.

Divers discovered another interesting object in the lazaret: a scoop pan balance scale that could probably hold up to thirty pounds.[6] A comparative study of scales of the period indicates the scale may be a crow's foot-style, single beam scale manufactured by the Fairbanks Company, although divers could not verify a manufacturer's name due to mussel cover. In 1824, two brothers, Erastus and Thaddeus Fairbanks, formed the E & T Fairbanks Company in St. Johnsbury, Vermont. Once in business together, the two brothers realized that the current weighing system yielded inaccurate results. In 1831 they patented a compound lever system attached to steelyard for balancing and indicating the weights. The steelyard had a sliding weight as well as hanging weights, like the ones on the wreck. By the time of the Civil War, Fairbanks scales were the best-known American product in the world. Considering its proximity to

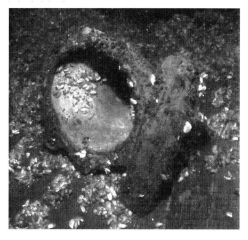

Period advertisements feature a toilet and scale similar to those found in the lazeret on the wreck. Photographs by Jeff Vos.

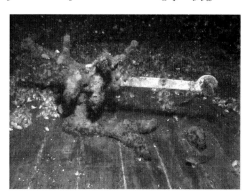

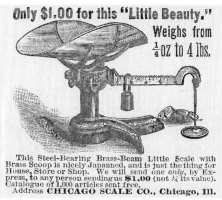

This cabin plan represents a possible layout for the cabin on the Hume. *It was developed by studying plans of similar vessels and observing conditions on the wreck. Drawing by Robert Doornbos.*

the cabin and galley, the scale may have been used to weigh ingredients used in preparing meals for the crew.

Once the team completed work on the outside of the vessel, divers moved inside to record artifacts. As they began to photograph and inventory the artifacts, the team developed a classification system. Primary artifact categories included ship equipment, operational tools, maintenance tools, navigational tools, galleywares, personal possessions, and unknowns, items that could not be identified without further study. Because of a limited field season, divers had to cut some corners in documentation. For instance, rather than triangulate the exact position of an artifact, divers noted only its general location. By saving time in that regard, they could spend more time looking at the objects and recording details. Had this site been much degraded, like the *Rockaway*, determining an exact spatial relationship would be necessary to understand the structure of the vessel. In this case, the vessel is so intact, that the team felt it safe to assume, for instance, that galleyware found under the cabin probably was once stored in the cabin.

The divers split into teams to record artifacts inside the vessel, one focusing on the bow and the other on the stern. Jeff Vos of MSRA, who was comfortable working in the dark, tight area of the forecastle below deck, took responsibility for meticulously photographing and detailing the artifacts in that area. The Chicago divers took the lead in documenting stern artifacts.

Divers worked on the cable tier, pictured above, to record a wide array of personal artifacts left behind by the crew. Bunks would have lined the walls just behind and on either side of the cable tier. A stove sat at the base of the sampson post, which still retains a metal cladding to protect it from the heat. Four men in a triangular space about ten feet by ten feet at its widest and longest points would have been very cramped. The drawing below depicts the probable layout for the forecastle on the Thomas Hume. *Photograph by Jeff Vos. Drawing by Robert Doornbos.*

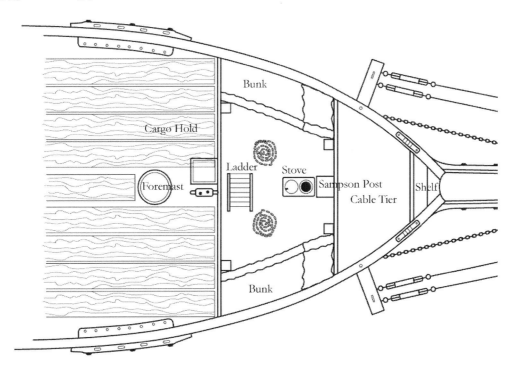

When the schooner capsized, the small box stove and firewood supply probably came loose and ended up on the cable tier along with many items of clothing. Photograph by Jeff Vos.

Documentation of the Forecastle Artifacts

Vos worked alone in the bow because the space was too tight to accommodate two divers. His dive partner would remain nearby doing other work or shooting video or still images. To access the bow, Vos swam down through the forward hatch in an area that would have been fully loaded with lumber had the vessel been carrying cargo. Based on the presence of a horizontal framing member below deck between the two small companionways behind the windlass, and broken timbers on the floor, it is believed that a wall existed at that spot dividing the crew's quarters from the cargo area. Therefore, the crew's only access to the forecastle would have been via a ladder through the forward companionway. Considering that this opening is too small for a diver with multiple tanks, it is fortunate the cargo wall no longer exists. Just forward of the place where the wall once stood, Vos filmed a length of anchor chain that runs down from the windlass through an opening in the deck and is coiled on the floor of the vessel within the forecastle. The small quarters would have felt even smaller

Found under the cable tier, this teakettle would have been used to boil water for coffee or tea. Apparently the crew had other "invigorating" drinks besides coffee and tea, based on the discovery of a wine bottle. Drawings by Valerie van Heest.

Found on the floor of the forecastle, this shovel and crock would have been usd by the crew. Photograph by Jeff Vos.

because the crew had to share living areas with storage space for the anchor chain. Several feet in front of this pile of chain is a triangular-shaped platform that fills the bow from side to side and from the stempost back about six feet to the sampson post. It is defined by maritime archaeologist David Cooper as a "cable tier," used, appropriately, for stowing cable. It is mounted about four feet above the floor of the vessel, creating a small space under the platform, likely for other types of storage. A smaller shelf above the cable tier has on it a piece of wire cable and a wooden block, perhaps stowed as spare rigging. Considering that the cable tier would have been built to hold heavy equipment, it is understandable why it has remained intact, when other structures are broken. In fact,

timbers scattered on the floor suggest, as do the plans from many schooners, that double-stacked bunks were once mounted on either side of the forecastle. In fact, there is just enough length from the cable tier back to where the wall once stood to accommodate the length of a man. Records indicate the *Hume* had a forecastle rebuild in the winter of 1884, so these structures may date to that period rather than its build in 1870.

The presence of clothing, shoes, small personal items, and a small one-burner box stove now littering the cable tier confirm that some of the *Hume* crew indeed bunked in the forecastle on the last run. Now on its side on the raised cable tier and with one leg broken off, the stove would have originally been secured to the floor in the center of the forecastle resting up against the sampson post. A vent pipe would have

A pair of machine-knitted socks, one loose sock, and two knit caps were found on the cable tier. Drawings by Valerie van Heest.

Although the thread of the seams had decayed, most of the individual pieces of a heavy wool jacket, as pictured in the advertisement above, remain on the cable tier. A variety of buttons and rivets was also found on the cable tier. Likewise, thread that held them to garments deteriorated leaving the buttons to fall loose. One button marked "Nicoll the Tailor" suggests that an expensive garment, perhaps the wool jacket was among the crew's possessions. Drawing by Valerie van Heest.

run up alongside the post and out through the deck above. In fact, a sheathing of some kind of lightweight metal on the sampson post, perhaps tin, confirms the position of the stove at its base. The metal would have protected the wooden post from the heat of the stove. The stove would have provided heat for the crew and allowed them to boil water or warm food. As confirmation of this, divers found a teakettle and a crock under the cable tier. A wine bottle found in the bow behind the cable tier suggests the crew might have had other beverages as well. Divers found a shovel that may have been used to empty ashes from the stove. Having food and drink in the bow may have been imperative because the only way to reach the galley would have been to cross the open deck, a dangerous endeavor in high waves that the crew might have chosen to avoid unless duty called.

Vos recorded the details of the clothing, shoes, and other personal articles on the cable tier surrounding the stove, prompting the team to determine if they could see anything resembling human remains. After several dives, they concluded there were no bones in the shipwreck. The crew would have been on deck working to save their vessel, not cowering in the forecastle. Throughout the dive season, Vos recorded details on a slate and made notations of the locations of all artifacts in the forecastle, spending up to fifty minutes per dive to accomplish this work.

Several garments on the cable tier are decayed beyond identification. One pile of darkened and worn semi-decayed fabric appears to have been a sweater, based on observation of woven light color strips of rubber band-like material that may have given the garment elasticity. Several pieces of a woven, denim-like material may have been the remnants of pants: They were long and narrow and had red threads, like pinstripes, down the length. A piece of dark cotton had a shape and buttonhole that suggested it may have been a vest. Other garments were quite distinct. Vos found a pair of socks, a single sock, two knitted caps, a bowler hat, and a single leather glove that appears to be a delicate men's dress glove, and not a heavy work glove as would be expected on a lumber schooner.

Two items of clothing on the cable tier are quite distinct. The first is a heavy wool jacket with three pockets: All of the pieces are extant; however, the threads of the seams and lining have decayed, leaving the garment in pieces. Likewise, another complete garment remains in pieces. The front, back and two short sleeves lay together, but the open weave fabric seems too delicate to have survived those many years. The team had trouble understanding what type of garment it was until LaFleur discovered a 1902 Sears catalogue that pictured an identical men's fishnet undershirt, advertised as the "coolest undershirt made."

Vos recorded a number of rivets that looked much like those fastened on jeans today, perhaps enough to have represented two or three pairs of pants. As with the garments, threads have decayed, leaving the rivets scattered. He also found several loose buttons, some white, one a bright blue, one wood, some metal, and two brass-colored stud-type buttons embossed with the name "Nicoll the Tailor." Discovering the name provides some insight into the garment from which it came. The October 30, 1878, *New York Times* provided a description of Alexander Nicoll and the garments he manufactured and sold.

The front, back, two sleeves, and facing of this fragile-looking garment lay on the cable tier. Divers were unsure what purpose this garment served until the discovery of the above 1902 Sears catalogue advertisement for "the coolest undershirt made." Drawing by Valerie van Heest.

"In a dingy little back office at No. 141 Bowery, sits, day after day, a white-haired old gentleman who manages the business of 42 merchant-tailoring establishments. The solitary window in the office lets in light from the courtyard of a large tenement house." The article explains that Nicoll has establishments in Boston, Philadelphia, Chicago, New Orleans, San Francisco, St. Louis, Cincinnati, Providence, and several other cities as well as eight tailoring shops in New York alone. Cloth is shipped to the Bowery address basement, then moved to another floor to be cut into patterns by hundreds of boys, then moved to an upper floor where men, boys and girls operate steam-powered sewing machines and sew the garments, which are then shipped to the

The shoe sits on top of the fabric that comprised the panels of the heavy wool suit jacket. Photograph by Jeff Vos.

42 different establishments throughout the Midwest and east ."[7]

Nicoll also produced custom garments. He could complete a pair of custom trousers in two and a half hours. His garments were high priced: Dress suits ranged from $25-$50, business suits from $12-$30, and overcoats from $10-$25. It seems possible that the Nicoll the Tailor button could be associated with the wool suit jacket. The jacket may have survived its long submersion nearly intact because of its quality.

Vos measured and photographed fifteen shoes in the forecastle that constituted four pairs and seven single shoes. It is possible that additional shoes remain hidden under boards in that area, perhaps enough to pair up the individual shoes. While most of the shoes appear to be heavy work shoes, one supple, leather loafer seems quite delicate. Another appears to be a dressy, wing-tip type of shoe.

Just a few items made of fabric were found buried in sand on the *Alvin Clark,* and *Rockaway.* The wealth of personal possessions and particularly clothes found on the *Lucerne* is more comparable to that found on the *Hume,* although there were significantly more items. Buried in the sand that filled the *Lucerne,* divers recovered hats, socks, vests, jackets, smoking implements, tools, paint cans, and brushes all similar style and vintage. However, the clothing on the *Hume* survived without being covered in sand. This fact is quite remarkable and warranted specific consideration. The divers noted that each time Vos emerged from working in the bow, he would find smear marks of a black, grease-like substance on his drysuit. It seemed possible that the marks were from the charred timbers he found, probably from in the stove, but on the surface, his suit smelled like petroleum. This gave rise to the suspicion that there may have been a container of oakum for caulking the hull or lubricant for the blocks or windlass kept in the forecastle. The suspicion regarding oakum is supported by the discovery of a caulking chisel and mallet in the forecastle. Perhaps the presence of that substance made the water less hospitable to waterborne bacteria that would normally have eaten away at fabrics such as those found on the cable tier.

Vos was also able to document meticulously several small, personal possessions scattered on the cable tier. A small cigar holder appears to be made of meerschaum with an amber tip. A short chain, a swivel-hinged locket, and a medallion all appear

Drawings of the shoes and their soles show the style, size, and condition. Pair P-2 is located in the stern and may have belonged to the captain, first mate, or steward. All other shoes are located in the forecastle. Shoe numbers R-1 and L-3 appear to be dress shoes. Perhaps a crewman brought these along for a special occasion. Notice shoes R-1, R-2, and R-3 appear to be the same size. Drawings by Valerie van Heest.

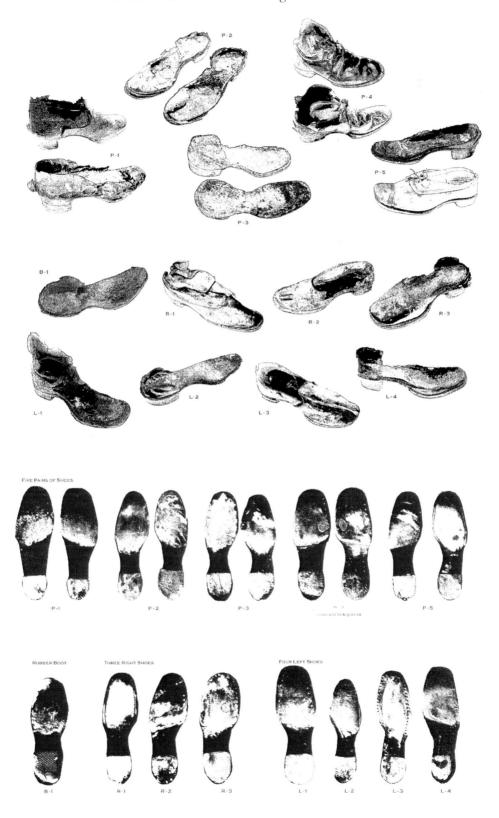

FIVE PAIRS OF SHOES

P-1   P-2   P-3   P-4   P-5

RUBBER BOOT   THREE RIGHT SHOES   FOUR LEFT SHOES

B-1   R-1   R-2   R-3   L-1   L-2   L-3   L-4

to be made of the same brass-like metal. (Gold would have remained shinier.) Although the items do not remain connected, they lie near each other and two of the three pieces are engraved with the same date and manufacturer: D. B. Castle and Co. September 1874. Later research discovered a similar locket, which has a tiger-eye cameo on one side and a small, flat piece of black onyx on the other. Had the locket on the wreck been opened, it would likely have revealed two glass panels for photographs. Daniel B. Castle had been a watchmaker and jeweler in New York with offices at 25 Main Street.[8] Obituary records show that he died of apoplexy at the age of seventy in 1883, with the status of being the oldest jeweler in New York at the time. The date and this information suggest that the locket and chain were among a crewmember's personal possessions and probably carried for a number of years, maybe even since new in 1874. It may have been part of a watch fob. A pocket watch likely remains hidden somewhere in the forecastle.

Vos found a curious artifact among the clothing on the cable tier: an iron cobbler's form. The leather glove had became partially affixed to it as the iron rusted. No records exist of a similar artifact on a schooner although it is not inconceivable that a crewman knew the cobbler's trade and repaired the shoes of fellow crewmen. Virtually all of the shoes on the wreck showed signs of significant wear on the soles. One pair of shoes found on the wreck had two distinct patches. Perhaps the cobbler-crewman repaired them as a side business.

Vos documented six coins scattered on the bow platform: two American, two Norwegian, one Dutch, and one Austrian. These coins suggest the crew hailed from a number of different countries, although it is just as likely the coins were used as regular currency at the time. A coin dealer suggested that low denomination coins of foreign currency were accepted in America, just as American businesses often accept Canadian coins today. These coins are indicative of the melting pot that was America at the time this vessel sailed.

Vos also found some thick pieces of leather on the cable tier. Careful observation revealed one to be a leather apron with a waist strap and buckles. It had a curved notch at what would have been the space between the legs. The other two pieces appear to be rigid leather thigh guards: They have retained the shape of a knee and thigh. Holes along the edges suggest that laces may have secured them to the leg. Discovery of a

Drawingss depict the detail a photograph cannot. A similar locket was found in an antique store and is pictured above. Drawings by Valerie van Heest.

These similar coins depict the type and denomination found on the wreck: 1883 and 1886 United States Indian head pennies on the left, an 1876 Norwegian 1 ore and an 1877 Norwegian 2 ore in the center, an 1860 Austrian 1 Kreuzer on the top right, and an 1875 Netherlands 1 cent on the bottom right. Van Heest collection.

photograph of shore-based dock wallopers (page 94), men who loaded and unloaded lumber schooners, gave rise to the possibility that at least one member of the crew may have participated in the cargo handling, an unexpected discovery considering the strong dock wallopers union at the time. The notch in the apron is different from the solid aprons seen on the dock wallopers. It may have been fashioned that way to allow the lumber handling crewman movement of his legs in order to climb in and out of the cargo hold. In light of the discovery of these lumber handling implements, the heaviest pair of leather work shoes (P-1 on page 91) found in the bow proved curious. Each shoe had a small solid leather nib affixed securely to the heel. Perhaps these shoes belonged to the same crewman who owned the apron and thigh guards. Such a nib may have allowed the wearer to raise a piece of lumber without having to bend over, but this is only speculation.

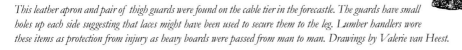

This leather apron and pair of thigh guards were found on the cable tier in the forecastle. The guards have small holes up each side suggesting that laces might have been used to secure them to the leg. Lumber handlers wore these items as protection from injury as heavy boards were passed from man to man. Drawings by Valerie van Heest.

Skilled lumber loaders called dock wallopers gathered in Muskegon in this 1890s photograph. Notice the man wearing the leather apron in back left and the man wearing thigh guards in the front right. These items are very similar to those found on the wreck. Lakeshore Museum Center Collection.

The Possibility of Passengers

By studying the wreck and the artifacts, the team hoped to determine whether the note found in the bottle indicating that the *Hume* "was drifting and taking on water," written by supposed passengers on the *Thomas Hume,* can be believed or whether it was a hoax. Although officials of Hackley & Hume denounced the bottle message as a hoax, schooners were like the Greyhound buses of their day and it was not uncommon for people to hitch a ride, particularly if a vessel was running empty.[9] One significant example of this is the *Rouse Simons,* which carried a number of lumberjacks along on its final run in 1912 in addition to its massive cargo of Christmas trees. Carrying passengers may not have been a practice supported by the ship owners, but could have been something the captains did for a few extra dollars. It is also interesting to note that less than a month after the sinking of the *Rouse Simmons,* a note in a bottle washed on the shore of Sheboygan, Wisconsin. It read, "Friday...everybody goodbye. I guess we are all through. During the night the small boat was washed overboard. Leaking bad. Ingvald and Steve lost too. God help us. Herman Schunemann."[10] No one has questioned the authenticity of that note written by the schooner captain: Writing such notes was a common practice on Great Lakes vessels in event of an emergency.

The presence of a large amount of clothing and potentially thirteen pairs of shoes on board the *Hume* for such a short run with a crew of seven gives rise to the possibility that there may really have been passengers on board. For short runs across the lake it would be uncommon for crewmen to bring a change of clothes. This is supported by the minimal clothing found buried in the silt on the *Alvin Clark*.[11] This

This view looks aft in the cargo hold from the starboard side of the centerboard trunk. In view are the two wooden upright supports that flank the fore and aft sides of the third hatch. The third upright is actually the base of the mizzenmast that used to pass through the cabin. Dozens of artifacts litter the floor of the cargo hold on the starboard side. These tools, galleyware, and some personal items would have been located in the cabin.

suggests that the crew of the *Clark* did not carry extra clothing with them on a run from Racine, Wisconsin, to Oconto, Michigan, and then down to Chicago, which would have taken about six days round trip, two days longer than the *Hume*'s regular trips.

The discovery of what may have been an expensive Nicoll the Tailor "designer" jacket, a dressy leather glove, a wing-tip shoe, and a casual loafer, all found in the crew's forecastle, may point to a passenger of loftier position than a crewman. Understanding that a crewman's salary averaged about $2 per day as compared to a captain who made about ten times that much, it would be hard to comprehend how a crewman could afford such fine garments. Additionally, the documentation of three vastly different style shoes all virtually the same size—a casual soft loafer, a wing tip, and a leather brogan—may indicate that they all belonged to one person, perhaps a passenger who carried with him several pair of shoes. Of course, it remains possible that a member or members of the crew were itinerant and carried all their possessions with them on board, or took extra clothing along for activities in port.

Besides the circumstantial evidence of clothing in the *Hume* that points to the possibility there were passengers on board, a genealogical search also lends some credence to the passengers being real. As will be recalled, the "passengers" Frank Maynard and Wilbur Grover had indicated that they had friends in McCook, Nebraska, and Elkhart, Indiana. If one accepts that the order of the names written matches the order of the towns written, then Maynard had friends in Nebraska and Grover had friends in Indiana. One could also assume both men were single or else they may have asked that wives be notified. The 1880 census records show only two men named Wilbur Grover living in the United States at the time. The first one, a six-year-old Wisconsin boy, would have been seventeen when the *Hume* sank. The second one, a nineteen-year-old, single druggist living in Tippecanoe, Indiana—a town about thirty miles south of Elkhart—would have been thirty-one when the Hume sank. The census showed the Indiana Grover living as a boarder in the house of the Williams family. Unfortunately, records from the 1890 census no longer exist due to an archives fire, so it cannot be determined where the two Wilbur Grovers then resided. Neither of these Grovers is listed in the 1900 census, suggesting that by then each may have died, one perhaps on the *Hume*. Unfortunately, the name Frank Maynard is too common to draw any conclusions from census records: Several dozen men of that name lived in various places in the country, but census records show none living in Nebraska during that period.

Documentation of Cargo Hold Artifacts

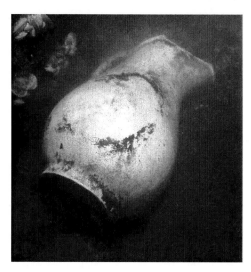

A white ceramic pitcher lies on its side and photographs show a blue substance around the opening. Without laboratory testing, the type of substance could not be determined. A second, almost identical, pitcher has a manufacturer's mark denoting that C. C. Thompson, an American pottery company, made the piece. Photography by Jeff Vos.

While Vos focused his work in the bow, Strunka worked at recording artifacts in the cargo hold. The space in the hold between the forecastle and the cabin, an area about eighty feet long, is virtually empty except for one ceramic pitcher up against the centerboard trunk on the port side. Strunka began finding artifacts under the floor of what had been the cabin at the sterncastle. These artifacts consist of galleyware, tools, and just a few personal items and are presumed to have fallen through the floor joists of the cabin floor when the cabin popped off during the sinking.

Strunka recorded a pair of leather shoes with the uppers missing, and the sole of a rubber boot. The boot had an oval-shaped logo on the bottom with a glove in the middle. Words across the top of the logo were obscured, but the words "New York" could be seen on the bottom side of the logo. An internet search turned up a pair of child's galoshes at an antique store. The identical logo revealed the words across the top: "Goodyear's Manufacturing Company." Rubber boots had early origins dating back to when Columbus reached the New World and observed natives playing games with a rubber ball. They collected the white latex sap of a rubber tree, dipped a stick in the sap, heated it over an open fire, and added layer upon layer until they had a black ball of rubber. Historians believe the men may have dipped their feet into the sap to create a form of a shoe. [12] However, not until 1823 would anyone attempt to use rubber in mass-production of boots. Charles Goodyear began experimenting with latex in 1823 and had an accidental production break-through in 1839 when, according to his own book, *Gum-Elastic and Its Varieties*, he spilled a mass of rubber, sulfur, and white lead onto a hot stove and witnessed the mixture charring around the edges but, surprisingly, not melting. Goodyear later fine-tuned the process and coined it "vulcanization." During the next thirty years, thousands of rubber products appeared, including boots that would become an important part of sailors' gear. The only other personal item in the stern is a bowler hat.

In addition to these few personal items, artifacts from a variety of different categories remain in the stern. Several tools lie scattered on the starboard side, including one piece of a three-piece taffrail log. The device, also called patent log or screw log, mechanically measured a vessel's speed. This taff rail log is made of three components: a cylindrical counter, a hard cable, and a torpedo-shaped apparatus with fins that is dragged from the stern of a vessel. The torpedo would have rotated as it was pulled through the water and a mechanical counter would have registered the rotation, thus determining the speed.

In addition to the numerous loose planks scattered on the floor of the vessel that may have been floorboards or interior walls, divers found other things that they believed to be part of the ship's structure: three porcelain doorknobs and a thirty-inch-long piece of wood with a white

A close-up photograph of the bottom of the rubber boot sole revealed a logo, with the name obscured but the words "New York" visible. Careful research identified the manufacturer as the Goodyear's Manufacturing Company. Photograph by Valerie van Heest.

Based upon the study of the taffrail rotator found on the wreck, it was manufactured by John Bliss & Company which bought the patent for the device from another designer and modified the rotator, patenting it in 1878. It is possible that the other half of the device, as pictured in a period advertisement below, still lies among the debris in the wreck. Drawing by Valerie van Heest. Advertisement courtesy of Norman Bliss.

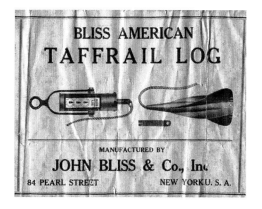

A mallet is just one of several tools found in the cargo hold beneath the cabin. Photograph by Robert Underhill.

The paintbrush appears little different from brushes today, although the bristles have became a hardened lump that appears to be caked with paint. Drawing by Valerie van Heest.

Two frying pans were found in the cargo hold below the cabin, one white enamel (left) and the other iron. Photograph by Robert Underhill.

ceramic knob. The piece of wood may have come from a screened cabinet or room door, based on impressions in the pattern of screening in the wood. A tiny area revealed a small bit of blue paint on it. Divers found two wood blocks, part of the ship's rigging. They may have been stowed below as extras, or used to move cargo inside the schooner, or even blocks that fell off the rigging during the sinking. Several maintenance tools remain, including a hammer, mallet, and a paintbrush complete with intact but worn and hardened bristles; only the wooden handle has partially deteriorated. Three lumps of some kind of material lie nearby, presumed to be clumps of semi-hardened paint. Although the clumps all appear dark in color, closer inspection revealed each to be a slightly different shade, possibly blue, green, and red, although it was difficult to tell with any kind of accuracy unless the material could be analyzed.

The largest single category of artifacts in the stern is associated with the galley. Among these items are plates, bowls, crockery, two pitchers, saucers, a black jug, a utensil, a white enamel-coated frying pan and an iron pan, and a white lump of what appeared to be food. The *Alvin Clark* had a crock of cheese still edible when recovered, which gives rise to the possibility that the lump of food on the *Hume* may also be cheese. Manufacturing logos are visible on three ceramic pieces.

As previously mentioned, the Chicago divers found a bowl with the logo of Royal Ironstone China Alfred Meakin England. Meakin founded his company in 1875 and operated under that name until 1897. According to an 1881 advertisement, Alfred Meakin manufactured ironstone china and white graniteware for export, using mail-order catalogues of large companies in the United States.[13] Sometime around 1891, the company began operating under Alfred Meakin, Ltd., changing the logo to add the limited designation. The company manufactured its wares at Highgate Potteries, on Parsonage Street in Tunstall, England.[14]

One of the two white pitchers has on its bottom the logo of C. C. Thompson. Cassius C. Thompson manufactured pottery in Liverpool, Ohio, under that name from 1868-1889, then added Pottery Company after its name through 1938.[15]

The third piece of china with manufacturing information is a plate with the name "Warranted Ironstone China John Edwards." This line began manufacture in the 1840s in England and undecorated wares like this plate were imported to the American and Canadian markets. In 1842, John Edwards marketed the first white ironstone china in America. Until the late nineteenth century, most dinnerware in the United States was imported, although a few companies like C. C. Thompson, mentioned above, manufactured their wares in the States.

The variety of different manufacturers of the dinnerware in the stern indicates that the vessel was old when it sank. The *Lucerne* revealed a similar collection of mismatched china, many from the same manufacturers that probably regularly supplied china for vessels. Whereas originally these schooners may have received a matching set of dishes, as the vessel aged, and things broke, its owners or captains would have outfitted it with whatever items they had on hand.

Only one item was found on the port side under the cabin floor: a small boat, sitting upright and near the keel. It measures less than ten feet long, although an exact measurement could not be taken because of

Several white ceramic plates, saucers and bowls were found in the cargo hold beneath the cabin. Some are broken, but others are in excellent condition, like the dinner plate and saucers above. A John Edward's manufacturers mark (below) appeared on one of the plates. Photograph by Robert Underhill.

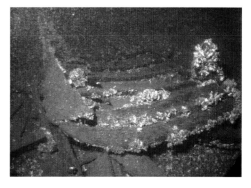

The remains of a small, much degraded boat lying on the starboard side of the cargo hold beneath the cabin may have been a dingy, stowed inside during travel. Crew might have used it for fishing while in port or for transport in the river. Photograph by Robert Underhill.

Artifacts in the cargo hold under the cabin include, from left to right, a mallet, wooden block, lamp part, hat, lamp globe, unidentified mass, and a wooden block. Photograph by Robert Underhill.

its broken condition. Only the frames of its lower structure are in place, and it seems there is a jumble of planks around it. Its presence inside the vessel is curious. Although Hume told reporters his schooner carried a newer yawl boat, the boat in the wreck appears too small to accommodate the entire crew, and, if stowed inside, would have been useless in an emergency.

Comparisons to Other Schooner Shipwrecks

Review of the hundreds of artifacts found on the *Alvin Clark,* now in the possession of the Detroit Historical Society, reveal that the *Hume* carried a similar collection of galleyware, tools, lamps, and personal items. For instance, the *Clark* had tools of all kinds and a paint bucket; the *Hume* had clumps of paint, a brush, and several maintenance tools. Both findings indicate that the crewmen did regular maintenance while on board their respective schooners.

Among the few schooner shipwrecks that have been well documented, the *Rockaway* offers the nearest comparison to the *Thomas Hume* with regard to size, vintage, and typical cargo. The 105-foot, two-masted scow schooner *Rockaway* was built in 1868 and sank in 1891, just a few months after the *Thomas Hume*. Both carried lumber during their final years. When found, the *Rockaway* was significantly broken up, but it is a testament to the skills of archaeologist Ken Pott that he could extract so much important data from the *Rockaway* and learn so much more about the operation and shipboard life of a lumber scow schooner. Two categories of artifacts on both shipwrecks are worthy of comparison: personal possessions and tools.

In this view panning right from the image on the opposite page, artifacts pictured here are some of the same items, plus a dark ceramic jug, a white pitcher, and a ceramic crock. Photograph by Robert Underhill.

The discovery of a pipe, a small piece of a vest, and a watch on the *Rockaway* are comparable to the personal possessions found on the *Hume*, although Pott attributed these items to the captain and mate since they were located nearer to the stern where people in those positions were typically housed. On the *Hume*, these items likely belonged to crewmembers because they were found in the bow. Likewise, divers found five shoes on the *Rockaway*, all lefts. Pott concluded that seamen may have removed one shoe (from their dominant foot) to afford better traction on the wet deck in a storm. The discovery of one lone rubber boot sole on the *Hume* confirms that such footwear did exist at that time and gives rise to the possibility that the crew of the *Rockaway* wore boots, leaving their leather shoes below deck. Perhaps it is just a coincidence that only the left shoes remained, the rights possibly carried away in the sinking.

Pott found a number of implements on the *Rockaway* that would have been used to load, unload, and move lumber on the vessel, like cant hooks with either short and extended handles and a pike pole; however, no such items have been found on the *Hume*. This, and the lack of any artifacts on board associated with the moving and stowing of lumber, could suggest that skilled dock wallopers in Muskegon and Chicago handled the loading and unloading of cargo. Only the presence of one leather apron, the pair of leather thigh guards, and the work shoes with the heel nibs suggest that a crewman on board the *Hume* may have participated in handling cargo. Considering the lack of iron tools for this work, it seems more likely the *Hume* crewman only supervised the loading, perhaps based on his familiarity with the layout of the *Hume*.

The divers recorded a tremendous amount of data during the 2010 field season.

Many of the same artifacts pictured on pages 100 and 101 can be seen here from a different angle. Photograph by Robert Underhill.

The team was able to accomplish all the major objectives and in fact had the time to document with some level of detail the structure of the vessel as well as a number of individual artifacts. Although the team recorded over one hundred artifacts during the 2010 investigations, the divers who spent the most time in the bow and stern estimate that at least that many artifacts may remain hidden below loose boards and under other artifacts. Lack of time and the inability to recover artifacts because of the constraints imposed by the state of Illinois have limited the team's ability to account completely for all the artifacts on the shipwreck. Although the artifact inventory of the *Hume* cannot be considered complete, it is curious that no personal grooming items were found, like the combs and toothbrushes on the *Alvin Clark* and *Lucerne*.

Vessel Identification

The team hoped to find positive proof of the identity of the sunken vessel during the archaeological investigation. The Chicago team based their identification in 2006 on circumstantial evidence including dimensions, an empty cargo hold, the rigging, and the manufacturing date of a bowl. Throughout the entire 2010 fieldwork season, divers continued to search for positive identification through registration numbers or an artifact with the name, but didn't find any such markings. Marine regulations required each vessel owner to carve its number and tonnage in the main beam. Although divers have found such numbers on wrecks such as the *Wells Burt* and others, more often they are not present. Archaeologists David Cooper and Wayne Lusardi both noted that they have seen few shipwrecks in which the number is present. This regulation was probably not strictly enforced. Despite no positive proof, the team concluded that the original identification as the *Thomas Hume* had been correct based on a plethora of circumstantial evidence. The vessel dimensions matched the enrolled dimensions of the *Thomas Hume* almost identically. The discovery of manufacturing marks on three ceramic pieces, a plate, and a pitcher, indicate they could have been produced before 1891. All six coins and the locket chain are dated prior to 1891, the "newest" coin from 1886, five years before the *Hume* sank. The presence of wire rigging and a steel stock anchor all suggest a vessel that operated significantly after the 1870s, and support the fact that the *Albrecht* was built with wire rigging. Considering the team could not find any reference to any other missing, three-masted, empty schooners in the range of 130 feet in all of Lake Michigan, the team concluded that the shipwreck is, in fact, the *Thomas Hume*.

Despite the recorded recollection of former crewmember Drumm of the *Hume* receiving a third mast, the fact that the *Hume*'s last enrollment in 1884 listed it as a two-masted schooner gave small concern that the wreck may not be the *Hume*. However, review of the Navigation Laws of the United States Bureau of Navigation, revised in 1886, indicates that re-enrollment is required if a vessel "is sold, altered in form or burden, lengthened or built upon, or from one denomination to another, by the mode or method of rigging or fitting." As long as the tonnage did not change, it seems that a new enrollment for the simple addition of a mast would not be required.

In addition to providing good evidence that the wreck is the *Thomas Hume*, the survey of the cultural material inside the shipwreck offers a view into the lives of the crew and the activities aboard ship. It also offers testament to the final hours on board the schooner before it disappeared without a trace, where it lay hidden for more than a century.

---

1   Law of the United States Regarding Admeasuremnt of Vessels, Section 44 of the Act of August 4, 1790.

2   Ibid.

3   Louden Wilson, *History of the Two-Mast Rig* (Unpublished), Page 100.

4   Email correspondence with Tamara Thompson, January 2011.

5   Maureen Francis, "The Flush Toilet: A Tribute to Ingenuity" (Mastersplumbers.com, undated)

6   Stan B. Hansen, "Book of Scales." (Unpublished, 2007).

7   *New York Times,* October 30, 1878.

8   The Jewelers' Circular and Horological Review, Volume 38 April 5, 1899.

9   Interview with David Cooper, January 2011

10 Rochelle Pennington, *The Historic Christmas Tree Ship: A True Story of Faith, Hope and Love.* (Wisconsin: Pathways Press, 2008).

11 Interview with Bud Brain, December 2010.

12 Joe Jackson, *The Thief at the End of the World: Rubber, Power, and the Seeds of Empire*, (New York: Penguin Group, 2008).

13 http://www.mygrannysatticantiques.com

14 http://www.thepotteries.org/allpotters/722.html

15 http://www.themuseumofceramics.org/pottery.html

A close-up view of the port steel-stock anchor.
Photograph by Robert Underhill.

Final Hours of the
THOMAS HUME

A more complete story of the *Thomas Hume*'s final trip and sinking can be understood by examining the historical and archaeological record, and ends— once and for all—the mystery of the schooner's disappearance. The discovery and identification of the *Thomas Hume* certainly rules out a collision, the suspected cause of the sinking. The orientation of the masts fallen to the starboard side on the wreck and the collection of artifacts on the starboard side of the cargo hold are indicative of capsizing, one of the possibilities that Charles Hackley and Thomas Hume considered at the time of the disappearance. However, they believed that had the *Hume* capsized, they would have found it still floating on the surface of the lake even days later.

Considering that the weather grew fierce that day in May, conditions on the lake probably played a significant role in the capsizing. However, unless the storm was more severe than any other weather the *Hume* had previously encountered, other factors probably contributed to its loss. Most accidents of any kind involve two or more things going wrong at the same time. Certainly, the fact that the *Hume* sailed home empty contributed in some way to the capsizing, In such a state, it would have sat higher out of the water exposing more surface area to the wind and making it less stable in big waves. However, the *Hume* had made over two hundred lake-crossings running light during its career for Hackley & Hume alone, undoubtedly many in bad weather. Something in addition to weather and the empty vessel must have led to the loss of the *Hume*. The answer may lie in the statement of *Hume* crewman Saxe Larson and in the note found three months later in the bottle. Larson indicated the *Hume* leaked badly that spring. The note indicated that the *Hume* was taking on water and drifting. Curiously, of the two bilge pumps on the deck of the *Hume*, the pump handle of one is missing and the pump handle of the other appears to have been in operation when it sank. A vessel riding light in a storm, with a leak, offers just the right combination of factors that could put the vessel in grave danger, particularly if a gale force gust hit the schooner. If, for some reason, the crew did not have the use of a lifeboat, then all hope for surviving a sinking in May in Lake Michigan would be lost. Through the study of the wreck and the historical record, a compelling scenario can be developed leading up to the disappearance of the *Thomas Hume*.

A Likely Scenario

By May 21, 1891, Captain Harry Albrightson had already made eight round trips of the season so far. His most recent trip had begun in Muskegon on May 19, when he sailed to Chicago in the company of the *Rouse Simmons*. The *Rouse Simmons* had been filled to capacity with a deck load on top of that: 306,000 board feet of lumber in total. The *Hume* had carried 236,000 board feet, and probably had only a small deck load. When the *Hume* reached the Chicago harbor sometime on May 20, Albrightson would have arranged a tow to Deming's yard at 236 South Water Street on the south branch of the Chicago River. Once his schooner was secured to the dock, Albrightson probably left the supervision of the unloading to his crew and the lumber in the care of Benjamin Deming, Hackley & Hume's agent in Chicago. He may have had the pleasure of spending the evening of May 20 at home with his wife and six children, although he would have had to find transportation there from the dock. From South Water Street, he would have to travel about five miles north on Halsted and about one mile west from Halsted on Avon (Chicago Avenue today) to his home at 36 Ayers Court. Most other *Hume* crewman probably slept at home that night as well. They all resided in Chicago. However, Albrightson probably left the schooner in the care of at least one crewman.

The weather that May had been rather normal for the spring.[1] Since the beginning of the month, the temperature warmed slowly, ranging from 35 degrees on May 1 to nearly 60 degrees near mid-May. Little if any rain fell during that period and winds were light. On that Thursday morning, the barometric pressure hovered just over 29

The Thomas Hume *would have been towed out of the Chicago River and into Lake Michigan on the morning of what turned out to be its final journey, like the* Apprentice Boy *pictured here being towed by the* J. C. Evans, *the former* James McGordon *of Hackley & McGordon. William Lafferty Collection.*

but had been falling steadily, indicating to a seasoned mariner like Albrightson that rain would be imminent. With humidity at 90 percent in Chicago that morning, the crew would have awakened to rain and may have gotten soaked getting back to the dock. They might have been pleased that the rain brought warming temperatures, which had reached 67 degrees by the early morning. However, the rain also brought with it a moderate breeze with signs of growing force. Crewman Saxe Larson may have had a good reason to be late to the dock that morning and miss the boat: He had sailed on the *Hume* several times that spring and took notice of a leak. Only one thing is certain: Larson's delay—whether intentional or not—saved his life.

Short one crewman, Albrightson may have been open to the proposition from two travelers asking if they might ride along to Muskegon. Anyone familiar with the comings and goings down at the lumber docks would know that at least one lumber schooner left those docks empty on a daily basis heading back to various ports along Michigan's western shore. Obviously, Captain Albrightson had no sense of impending doom. Just after dawn, clouds were heavy, and overnight the barometer rose, indicating colder temperatures and possible clearing. The wind blew at fourteen miles per hour out of the south with occasional gusts.[2] This moderate breeze would have generated waves only about one to three feet high and so the Chicago weather station officials would have had no reason to raise a flag of caution that morning.

Weather prediction was still in its infancy in 1891. While newspapers had long reported weather after it happened, it would take until the 1850s before anyone thought to use past data to generate predictions. Even then support for a weather forecasting service was not strong. Mariners, whose work depended on the weather did not expect the benefits to exceed the costs of establishing the network necessary to provide useful weather information.[3] It would take until 1870 for President Ulysses S. Grant to sign a bill establishing a meteorological observation network that would provide notice on the Great Lakes of the approach and force of storms.[4] The storm-warning system began formal operation in 1871 with planned flag displays at eight ports on the Great Lakes. The method of warning ships of dangerous winds would be to hoist a single red flag with a black square located in the middle as a cautionary signal whenever the winds were expected to be as strong as twenty-five miles per hour, and to continue so for several hours, within a radius of one hundred miles from the station. By 1891, three stations near Lake Michigan provided weather observations and mariner warnings: Chicago, Milwaukee, and Escanaba.[5] What none of the observers at these stations could know for certain is what kind of weather a vessel would experience out on the lake. The weather reported at port locations, including wind velocity and direction, humidity, barometric pressures, and temperature, would have been somewhat different than the weather actually occurring on the lake, but the reports would certainly provide some gauge regarding lake conditions.

Seeing no flags of caution and with years of experience sailing and watching the Lakes for signs of bad weather, Captain Albrightson probably saw no reason that his schooner could not make the trip. William Miller, the captain of the *Rouse Simmons,* obviously concurred because both captains arranged for tug boats to tow them up the river to the mouth about five miles distant, a trip that would have taken over an hour. Once out of the harbor, both schooners raised their sails as they headed northeast toward Muskegon.

On May 21, 1891, the weather in Chicago began to change drastically just a few hours after the *Hume* and the *Simmons* left Chicago, making conditions on the lower half of Lake Michigan less than optimal for sailing. However, farther north in Muskegon, the same rain did not bring with it the gusts that Captain Albrightson was likely experiencing on the lake, leaving Hackley & Hume officials oblivious to conditions their vessels were experiencing farther south. At some point during that Thursday out on the lake, rain fell in torrents in some places. The winds began to clock around toward the west, shifting quickly to the northeast and increasing to 25 to 34 miles per hour. This wind shift made temperatures drop quickly, sending colder air down from the north. Waves would have built steadily and grown severe by the time the *Thomas Hume* reached mid-Lake Michigan. The worsening winds and growing size of waves are what likely prompted Captain Miller of the *Rouse Simmons* to turn around and head back to take shelter in Chicago. Hackley & Hume gave its captains permission to make whatever decisions were necessary to insure the safety of the crew and the vessels. However, Albrightson maintained his course.

When the wind shifted to the northeast, Captain Albrightson would have found conditions impossible to sail directly into the wind on a northeast heading toward Muskegon. To avoid his sails luffing and inability to make headway northeast, he would have had to tack back and forth from east to west to attempt to reach Muskegon. However, by that point, he may have realized the severity of the weather and redirected his efforts at saving his boat rather than staying on course. Considering the northeast wind direction, he would likely have found making a turn back to Chicago and trying to sail southwest too dangerous. Even if he could manage the risky 180-degree turn, sailing with the wind at his stern would make steering difficult especially in rough water, and would increase the danger of the sails whipping quickly to the other side of the boat when least expected. Instead, he may have opted to tack to starboard and head east toward Michigan's shore to take shelter in the lee of the land. From there, if conditions improved, he could attempt to tack west and keep working his way north to Muskegon. Whatever he decided, he would have certainly conveyed it to the crew. Word on a small schooner would have spread quickly.

If the crew had not already donned their rubber work boots in Chicago, they would have done so at this point, stowing their leather shoes in the crew's area in the forecastle or rooms in the cabin. The northeast winds should have provided good conditions for sailing toward St. Joseph, but because the *Hume* never made it there, it evidently encountered other problems. It is possible that a severe wave could have torn the ship's wheel from the steering mechanism, rendering the ship unmanageable. In that event, it would have quickly turned sideways to the wind, a dangerous position. Riding high out of the water, as it did running empty, it would have capsized immediately, washing the crew into the water with little time to prepare an escape such as in the yawl boat. However, if this were the case, then there would not have been enough time to write a note, put it in a bottle, and toss it into the water.

It seems more likely that Captain Albrightson ordered the sails lowered in the face of the growing northeast wind. Without canvas, the *Hume* would not be able to make much headway, but the crewmen handling the helm may have still been able to control the vessel using the surface of the hull and the force of the wind on the port quarter to maintain the bow heading into the wind. In this position, the boat could have drifted south but stayed afloat. With winds reaching over 35 miles per hour that afternoon, waves would have washed over the deck, mostly running out through the continuous gap between the deck and the rail. But some water may have poured through the forward companionway into the forecastle and into the three cargo hatches even with the wooden covers secured. If the *Hume* had leaked on a calmer day earlier that season, the pounding of the waves would have stressed the then twenty-one-year-old hull even more. If the crew did not do it on their own, Albrigtson would have ordered them to the forward and amidships bilge pumps. With one man on each side, four of the crew would have been busy continuously pumping the rocker up and down, sucking water up through pipe that reached down into the bilge and discharging it onto the deck to run off. But in rolling seas, some of that pumped water could have found its way back inside the vessel. It is possible the crew could not keep up with the leak. Albrightson may have tried to calm his crew by sharing their current position near the St. Joseph course—a direct line between Chicago and St. Joseph, Michigan—and ordering them to keep working the pumps to give them enough time to reach the shelter of the land, only about twenty miles distant. But to be safe, he may have ordered the one or two crewmen not on the pumps to ready the yawl in case the *Hume* foundered. With so few crew to handle the davits, a wave could have easily torn the boat from their grip, sending it smashing into the violent water. At that point, all hope of escape would have been lost. The crew probably realized that the May water was too cold for them to survive. The two passengers, who may have been assisting in some way on deck, probably retreated to the shelter of the cabin to ponder the situation. Since their lake crossing was not a regularly scheduled passenger trip, there would be no record of their presence on board the *Hume*. They may have realized that their friends would never know what became of them if they perished on the lake. Frank Maynard may have decided to write a note indicating the hopelessness of the situation, their location, and their request to notify friends of their fate. While he did that, Wilbur Grover probably grabbed a half-full bottle from the galley, maybe took a swig of its contents, dumped out the rest, and jammed the note inside. One of them probably opened the cabin door, and hurled the bottle into the water. Even after that, they may have held onto the hope that Albrightson might somehow get the *Hume* to safety.

As the vessel struggled to hold its own in the storm, a massive wave may have torn off the wheel, putting the schooner at the mercy of the winds. Even if the vessel retained its wheel, a strong gale force gust of wind may have toppled the top-heavy vessel and forced it onto its starboard side, knocking everyone off their feet, some into the frigid water. Everything inside the cabin, cargo hold, and forecastle tumbled in the direction of the fall, including the heavy iron cook stove, which would have crashed though the

wall of the captain's room. The rudder would have also fallen in the same direction as the schooner rolled. With the port side of the schooner facing upward to the sky, the hull may have maintained equilibrium for a few minutes. The hull may even have supported a few of the crew as they struggled to avoid the water and evaluate their options for survival. One or two men might have made it onto the port side of the cabin, which may have kept them a few feet above the water's surface. As the cabin filled with water, broken floorboards, interior partitions, and furniture would have floated off, carried in various directions by the churning water along with buoyant objects in the cabin like clothing, food, and anything small and wooden. Heavier items like the dishes, tools, toilet, stove, and scale would have lain up against the starboard wall. As the weight of the incoming water began to pull the schooner lower in the water, air pockets inside the cargo hold and cabin would have forced the hatches and structure off the sinking vessel, creating an explosion of wooden timbers and snapping the mizzenmast off at the level of the deck.

Inside the forecastle, the small but heavy iron box stove ripped off its mount and crashed into the bunks on the starboard side, breaking off one of its legs in the process. The inrush of water from the companionway hatch forced it forward onto the cable tier, commingling with chain, tools, clothing, shoes, lamps, and crocks all caught in the whirlwind of water. A brass pocket watch, chain, and locket probably tore apart in the swirling waters.

For several minutes, the three masts held fast to the schooner as they churned on

An artist's rendering recreates the various stages of the Hume's *final hours, sailing, taking down the sails, capsizing, sinking, and settling on the bottom. Drawings by Robert Doornbos.*

the surface of the lake. The rigging still secured them perpendicular to the deck. As the vessel sank lower and lower and filled completely with water, the hull would have begun to right itself to its normal position, but the masts would have been too heavy to come up with the hull. The mast cap that joined the lower masts to the top masts would have snapped and the top masts floated off. At that point, the lower portion of the foremast and main mast fell off their steps but remained connected to the ship by the rigging, as did the broken mizzenmast. They would have been dragged down with the hull.

Once the vessel and the masts disappeared from the surface, the plunge to the bottom would have been quick. The centerboard hit the hard bottom and retracted into its box. The cast iron galley stove rolled back toward the middle of the cabin floor, settling into the opening in the floor of the cabin through which the mast used to pass. It would have crashed through the floor joists had the lower piece of the broken mizzenmast not supported it. As the masts settled perpendicular to the bottom, their bases wedged under the deck and their buoyancy cushioned the blow against the starboard rail so that they only slightly dented the rail. The mizzenmast rolled forward from its position over the area where the cabin had been and the gaffs and booms from all three masts broke, settling onto the deck or off in the sand to the starboard side.

After the *Hume* hit bottom, anyone left alive in the water would have been stunned and struggling. In May, the temperature of the water would have been somewhere between forty and forty-five degrees. The initial shock of the cold water would have placed severe strain on their bodies, driving their breath out upon impact with the water. If a man involuntarily gasped for breath while his head was still underwater, he would quickly drown. Certainly, cardiac arrest induced by the immediate cold could have taken a life or two. If any timbers floated in the area, the survivors may not have had the strength or mental faculties to reach them. Total disorientation can occur after cold-water immersion. It may have taken some of the men thrashing in the water thirty seconds or more to get their bearings. If anyone survived the sinking, his extremities would have numbed to the point of uselessness. Within minutes, severe pain would have clouded rational thought. Cold water would have robbed their bodies of heat much faster than the air. They would have begun to shiver almost immediately. Once their core temperature reached about 94 degrees, delirium would set in. In May, robust men might expect to survive in the water for thirty minutes. Their heads, necks, armpits, chests, and groins would lose heat fastest. Even if some of the men huddled in a group to try to maintain body heat, probably not easy in the high waves, strong, healthy, good swimmers could possibly last up to one hour while treading water. However, once body temperature lowered to 86 degrees, they would lose consciousness. Once their body temperature reached about 79 degrees, they would die. Even if a crewman had managed to climb onto a floating object, he could not expect to survive more than two to three hours. It is unlikely that any of the *Hume*'s crew lasted long that cold, stormy May day.

After a person dies in water, the body sinks because its specific gravity is very close to that of water. Sinking to the bottom, in this case probably 150 feet, bodies would drift along the sand bottom with the currents until putrefactive gases formed in the tissues decreasing the gravity of the body and creating sufficient buoyancy to allow it to rise to the surface and float. However, heavy clothing, like that which the crew of the *Hume* must have worn, may have delayed or even prevented the rise of the bodies. Considering that putrefaction proceeds at a slower rate in deep, cold water, conditions may have minimized the decay to the point that the bodies of the *Hume*'s victims may never have surfaced, instead being nibbled on by fish and decomposing underwater over time. This may be why no bodies from the *Hume* were ever recovered in the days, weeks, and months after the accident.

Although Hackley & Hume initiated several attempts in May and June 1891 to find the hull of the *Thomas Hume*, its final resting place, far off the normal course line between Chicago and Muskegon, served to help keep it hidden well into the twentieth century.

---

1 National Climactic Data Center Monthly Weather Records, Chicago, Illinois, May 1891.

2 Ibid.

3 Erik D. Craft, "Economic History of Weather Forecasting," October 6, 2001. http://eh.net/encyclopedia/article/craft.weather.forcasting.history.

4 Report of the Secretary of War Volume I, (Washington Government Printing Office 1871).

5 Erik D. Craft, "Economic History of Weather Forecasting," October 6, 2001, http://eh.net/encyclopedia/article/craft.weather.forcasting.history.

The location of the wreck in the southern basin of Lake Michigan about 24 miles from Chicago confirms Benjamin Deming's 1891 position that the Hume sank about twenty miles from Chicago. The fact that the wreck lies near the St. Joseph course line substantiates the suspicion that the Hume may have taken passengers aboard. A note supposedly written by two passengers on the Hume, found in a bottle three months after the disappearance, indicated the vessel was taking on water and drifting near the St. Joseph course.

CONCLUSION

Lingering MYSTERIES

The conclusions drawn about the identity of the shipwreck, life aboard the ship, the potential of passengers, and the circumstances that conspired to sink the *Thomas Hume* have been made in the context of both historic research and archaeological evidence. Although there may be several alternative ways of interpreting the evidence, none can ever be proven. As hard as archaeologists work to attempt to give voice to shipwrecks and artifacts, the fact remains they are inanimate objects incapable of communication. The words of Lee Murdock's song, "I'm Still Here," inspired when he saw the first underwater footage of the *Thomas Hume,* are the closest to imagining what the shipwreck might have to say. The three-masted lumber schooner once owned by Hackley & Hume is still *right there* on the bottom of Lake Michigan, just where it came to rest in 1891.

Aside from stepping into a time machine and traveling back to the decks of the *Thomas Hume* on that day in May 1891, the research about its career and the study of its physical remains will have to suffice to provide insights into the use of the vessel and the lives of the ordinary men who sailed it. The study of this shipwreck finally lays to rest the mysteries surrounding the sinking of the *Thomas Hume.* Although Thomas Hume and Charles Hackley could not imagine their vessel succumbing to the lake, the indisputable fact is that it did just that. Lake Michigan as well as the other four Great Lakes has a deadly history.

Oddly, despite all the mysteries that arose in the wake of the *Hume's* disappearance, the opinion expressed by Benjamin F. Deming in Chicago a week after the accident was right on target: "It is thought the catastrophe occurred within 20 miles of Chicago, and that the wreck must have dragged toward the head of the lake."[1] Had global positioning systems existed in 1891, Deming may have been able to put searchers near the very spot: The wreck rests about 24 miles from Chicago. It is possible that Captains Christian and Lee may have unknowingly steamed right over the sunken wreck in early June when they sailed from Chicago to St. Joseph looking for debris from a possible collision. In fact, any wooden debris from the vessel would have been pushed in many different directions by the currents, leaving no evidence at the scene of the catastrophic accident. In time, debris would have become waterlogged and eventually sink.

Some people may still be skeptical about the presence of passengers on a commercial schooner. A reporter editorialized soon after the bottle surfaced that he believed the note to be a hoax, explaining that he could not understand how a passenger from Nebraska or Indiana could know what course the ship sailed, specifically the "St. Joseph Course." Charles Hackley felt the same way, indicating his captains never took aboard passengers.[2] However, in plotting the final location of the *Thomas Hume* on a lake chart, it is immediately apparent that the wreck lies less than a half mile south of a direct line between the mouth of the Chicago harbor and the mouth of the St. Joseph harbor: in other words, on the St. Joseph course. Although stories abound of messages in bottles, some true and some pranks, it certainly seems probable that Frank Maynard and Wibur Grover's last written words explained exactly what befell the *Thomas Hume*, its passengers, and crew. The archaeological study of the wreck supported this.

Most archaeological projects of this size and magnitude take place over multiple years. In this particular time of economic challenges, the major grant from the Michigan Humanities Council made this project possible. Funds simply would not have existed to spend any more time on the project. Fortunately, the dedicated team was able to accomplish more than would typically be expected with such a tight schedule. Even with the limitations imposed by the state of Illinois, the team extracted an enormous amount of information from the shipwreck. However, for as many questions as the survey and research answered, that many new questions have arisen. Although the archaeological team has provided theories to answer some of these questions, there is the possibility of misinterpretation. Why are there at least thirteen pairs of shoes on the wreck, when there were only seven crew? Was the note in a bottle real or just a hoax? Why is there a beautiful man's jacket on board the schooner possibly made by a famous and expensive haberdasher? What is a cobbler's tool doing on board the *Thomas Hume*? Why are the coins from four different countries? Why did Captain Albrightson continue on when the *Rouse Simmons* turned back? Did the crew really launch the yawl? As Murdock's song reminds us, the *Thomas Hume* is still there and may be able to answer more questions, if curiosity persists.

Perhaps this project will inspire other divers, historians, and archaeologists to tackle in-depth shipwreck investigations. The data these wrecks can contribute is great and, in time, perhaps state governments responsible for the care of shipwrecks will find a way to work better with those willing to expend the time and money to properly document them. Many dedicated individuals share goals for the responsible study and preservation of these cultural resources. Many more members of the public can be inspired through the interpretation of these shipwrecks' histories and mysteries.

The artifacts that lie below the deck in the *Thomas Hume* are *extraordinary* because they are *ordinary*. These shoes, garments, tools, dinnerware, and a toilet, among other things, are just commonplace objects people used more than a century ago: They are little different from the same type of objects in use today. However, the fact that they have survived underwater for over 120 years is amazing! Each item provides silent testimony from the crew. The man who tied the knot on the wing-tip shoe reminds us that we will each tie our final knot. The people who tucked the locket, cigar holder, and coins away for safekeeping make us realize that we cannot take our most precious possessions with us after death. And, the legacy of the shipwreck makes us wonder what legacy we will leave long after we are gone.

APPENDIX

Shipping
LOGS

The Michigan State University Archives holds in its records the Hackley and Hume Papers from 1859 to 1955. These documents include correspondence, land patents, log receipts, financial material, and other records of J. N. Hackley & Company (1859-66), Hackley & Sons (1866-77), Hackley & McGordon (1866-80), C. H. Hackley & Company (1876-86), and Hackley & Hume (1881-1905). Also included are papers relating to investments of the family of Thomas Hume, including the holding companies Thomas Hume & Company (1907-54) and Hume, Hefferan & Company (1907-42), and material on lands in North Carolina and California, particularly redwood forests of the Sierra Nevada Mountains; probate reports, court orders, bequests, and other estate papers of Charles Henry Hackley, Thomas Hume, their families and business partners. Among the most important records relative to the vessel *Thomas Hume* are leather bound log books in which the details of each cargo shipment were kept, including the vessel name, date of shipment, amount of lumber, from where it was cut and to whom it was shipped. For the purposes of this publication, only the shipments on board the *H. C. Albrecht/ Thomas Hume* have been included. Study of these records has provided insights into the career of the *Thomas Hume*. Because these records have been transcribed from the hand writing of a variety of individuals, errors are possible.

LUMBER SHIPMENTS ON ALBRECHT/HUME

DATE	BOARD FEET 1000s	WHERE CUT	CONSIGNEE	DATE	BOARD FEET 1000s	WHERE CUT	CONSIGNEE
1878				10/30/1878	212.221	CHH&Co	Deming
4/18/1878	150.385	CHH & Co	Deming	10/30/1878	2.486	CHH&Co	Deming
4/18/1878	94.503	CHH&Co.	Deming	10/30/1878	4.16	CHH&Co	Deming
4/18/1878	94.503	CHH&Co	Deming	11/4/1878	157.943	CHH&Co	Coburn & Co
4/18/1878	150.385	CHH&Co	Deming	11/4/1878	60	BN&Co	Coburn & Co
4/22/1878	15.422	B N & Co.	Deming	11/8/1878	216.2133	CHH&Co	Deming
4/22/1878	66.637	CHH & Co	Deming	11/13/1878	218.616	CHH&Co	Deming
4/22/1878	53.325	CHH & Co	Deming	11/18/1878	79.767	CHH&Co	Deming
4/22/1878	86.466	BN&Co.	Deming	11/25/1878	211.2	CHH&Co	Deming
4/22/1878	154.22	BN&CO.	Deming	11/25/1878	25.848	CHH&Co	Deming
4/22/1878	66.637	CHH&Co.	Deming	11/29/1878	192.7	CHH&Co	Deming
4/22/1878	53.325	CHH&Co.	Deming	11/29/1878	45.314	CHH&Co	Deming
4/25/1878	209.268	CHH&Co.	Deming	1879			
4/25/1878	6.933	CHH&Co.	Deming	4/15/1879	263.606	CHH&Co	Deming
4/25/1878	89.79	CHH&Co.	Deming	4/24/1879	224.214	CHH&Co	Deming
5/7/1878	230.37	CHH&Co	Deming	5/1/1879	220.615	CHH&Co	Deming
5/18/1878	233.938	CHH&Co	Hanly	5/7/1879	261.871	CHH&Co	Deming
5/22/1878	233.568	CHH&Co	Hanly	5/10/1879	233.216	BN&Co	Colburn Jones & Co.
5/25/1878	236.816	CHH&Co	Hanly	5/14/1879	263.268	CHH&Co	Deming
5/29/1878	236.131	CHH&Co	Hanly	5/17/1879	239.227	CHH&Co	Deming
6/1/1878	234.941	CHH&Co	Hanly	5/22/1879	225.232	CHH&Co	Deming
6/10/1878	237.356	CHH&Co		5/26/1879	233.942	CHH&Co	Deming
6/15/1878	236.422	CHH&Co	Hanly	5/31/1879	250	CHH&Co	Deming
6/20/1878	234.237	CHH&Co	Hanly	6/4/1879	250	CHH&Co	Deming
6/24/1878	237.032	CHH&Co	Hanly	6/21/1879	242.3	CHH&Co	
6/29/1878	238.343	CHH&Co	Hanly	6/28/1879	242.881	CHH&Co	Deming
7/4/1878	210.659	CHH&Co	Deming	7/1/1879	246.502	CHH&Co	Deming
7/12/1878	239.383	CHH&Co.	Deming	7/8/1879	236.31	CHH&Co	Deming
7/17/1878	164.962	CHH & Co	Deming	7/14/1879	235.982	CHH&Co	Deming
7/17/1878	86.163	CHH&Co	Deming	7/19/1879	121.465	CB&Co	Deming
7/22/1878	235	CHH&Co	Ewing	7/19/1879	136.706	CB&Co	Deming
7/25/1878	242.611	CHH&Co	Ewing	7/26/1879	222.277	CHH&Co	Deming
7/31/1878	240	CHH&Co	Ewing	7/26/1879	11.088	CHH&Co	Deming
8/3/1878	200	CHH&Co	Ewing	7/31/1879	174.421	CHH&Co	Coburn & Co
8/10/1878	99.465	CHH&Co	Coburn & Jones	8/5/1879	263.613	CHH & Co	
8/10/1878	153.058	CHH&Co	Coburn & Jones	8/11/1879	231.77	CHH&Co	Coburn Jones & Co
8/14/1878	220	CHH&Co	Ewing	8/16/1879	208.334	CHH&Co	A N Gray Co.
8/19/1878	265.272	CHH&Co	Deming	8/20/1879	250	CHH&Co	Deming
8/23/1878	256.124	CHH & Co	Deming	8/25/1879	136.883	CHH&Co	W. Shoemaker
8/23/1878			see H Tully	8/28/1879	238.308	CHH&Co	Meglade
8/29/1878	243.313	CHH&Co	Deming	9/1/1879	226.58	CHH&Co	A N Gray Co.
9/7/1878	123.215	BN&Co.	Deming	9/5/1879	229.436	CHH&Co	Shoemaker
9/12/1878	239.453	CHH&Co	A M Colborn	9/10/1879	156.652	CHH&Co	Shoemaker
9/16/1878	242.619	CHH&Co	Deming	9/15/1879	226.436	CHH&Co	A N Gray Co.
9/23/1878	219.35	CHH&Co	Ewing	9/19/1879	256.962	CHH&Co	Deming
9/26/1878	234.753	CHH&Co	Deming	9/24/1879	256.93	CHH&Co	Deming
9/30/1878	231.1	CHH&Co	Deming	9/27/1879	248.9	CHH&Co	Deming
10/5/1878	203.358	CHH&Co	Deming	10/1/1879	232.472	CHH&Co	Adams & Lord
10/9/1878	230.758	CHH&Co	Deming	10/6/1879	219.146	CHH&Co	Sopie & Pash Co
10/17/1878	178.446	CHH&Co	Deming	10/10/1879	202.264	CHH&Co	Shoemaker
10/17/1878		CHH&Co	Deming	10/10/1879	196.06	CHH&Co	Shoemaker
10/21/1878	158.3	CHH&Co	Coburn & Co	10/15/1879	70.346	CHH&Co	Deming
10/26/1878	208.475	CHH&Co	Deming	10/15/1879	181.073	CHH&Co	Deming
10/26/1878	3.387	CHH&Co	Deming	10/18/1879	221.161	CHH&Co	T Wilco Co

LUMBER SHIPMENTS ON ALBRECHT/HUME

DATE	BOARD FEET 1000s	WHERE CUT	CONSIGNEE	DATE	BOARD FEET 1000s	WHERE CUT	CONSIGNEE
10/22/1879	224.565	CHH&Co	S K Martin	9/29/1880	220.063	CHH&Co	Streek C & Keep
10/27/1879	221.532	CHH&Co	Ambrose	10/4/1880	221.877	CHH&Co	Streek C & Keep
11/1/1879	121.857	CHH&Co	Shoemaker	10/8/1880	249.591	CHH&Co	Deming
11/6/1879	118.145	CHH&Co	Shoemaker	10/13/1880	214.244	CHH&Co	Streek C & Keep
11/6/1879	92.411	CHH&Co	Shoemaker	10/16/1880	221.76	CHH&CO	Deming
11/11/1879	121.665	CHH & Co	Tyson	10/25/1880	216.906	CHH&Co	Deming
11/15/1879	219.009	CHH&Co	Deming	10/29/1880	249.498	CHH&Co	Deming
11/20/1879	133.07	CHH&Co	Shoemaker	11/3/1880	150.337	CHH&Co	Deming
11/20/1879	78.638	CHH&Co	Shoemaker	11/8/1880	251.015	CHH&Co	Deming
11/26/1879		CHH&Co	Bryant	11/13/1880	216.143	CHH&Co	Deming
11/26/1879	161.728	CHH & Co	Tyson	**1881**			
1880				4/26/1881	244.527	CHH&Co	W. Shoemaker
4/27/1880	24.346	CHH&Co	Tyson	4/30/1881	248.821	CHH&Co	W. Shoemaker
4/27/1880	84.825	CHH&Co	Tyson	5/19/1881	188.007	CHH&Co	Soper Bros
4/27/1880	101.049	CHH&Co	Tyson	5/19/1881	3.867	CHH&Co	Soper Bros
4/30/1880	221.266	CHH&Co	Deming	5/26/1881	223.594	CHH&Co	Soper & Pond
5/5/1880	147.264	CHH&Co	Ambrose & Brooks	5/26/1881	1.108	CHH&Co	Soper & Pond
5/5/1880	104.769	CHH&Co	Ambrose & Brooks	6/4/1881	231.677	CHH&Co	S C Martin
5/8/1880	192.689	CHH&Co	Deming	6/11/1881	99.663	CHH&Co	S C Martin
5/8/1880	59.865	CHH&Co	Deming	6/11/1881		CHH&Co	S C Martin
5/13/1880	217.917	CHH&Co	Ambrose	6/18/1881	179.391	CHH&Co	W. Shoemaker
5/13/1880	3.667	CHH&Co	Ambrose	7/1/1881	104.399	CHH&Co	Chese & Pato
5/17/1880	219.761	CHH&Co	Ambrose	7/7/1881	187.906	CHH&Co	Soper Bros
5/20/1880	219.971	CHH&Co	Ambrose	7/20/1881	62.321	CHH&Co	W. Shoemaker
5/24/1880	219.185	CHH&Co	Ambrose	7/20/1881	168.905	CHH&Co	W. Shoemaker
5/27/1880	226.821	CHH&Co	Shoemaker	7/28/1881	204.01	Hamilton	WM & Co.
5/31/1880	221.375	CHH&CO	Deming	7/28/1881	68.43	Beidlie	WM & Co
6/4/1880	219.587	CHH&Co	Ambrose	8/6/1881	172.21	CHH&Co	W M Co.
6/12/1880	211.221	CHH&Co	Ambrose	8/9/1881	231.537	CHH&Co	Soper
6/17/1880	229.191	CHH&Co	Ambrose	8/17/1881	25.598	Wayens	RR & Co
6/17/1880	229.191	CHH & Co	Ambrose	8/23/1881	230.228	CHH&Co	Soper
6/23/1880	228.745	CHH & Co	Ambrose	8/26/1881	160.348	CHH&Co	W. Shoemaker
6/29/1880	233.772	CHH & Co	Ewing	8/26/1881	41.267	CHH&Co	W. Shoemaker
7/1/1880	222.654	CHH & Co	Martin	8/26/1881	54.115	CHH&Co	W. Shoemaker
7/5/1880	199.306	CHH&Co	Shoemaker	8/30/1881	234.84	CHH&Co	
7/5/1880	48.83	CHH&Co	Deming	9/5/1881	199.323	CHH&Co	S L Penny
7/8/1880	232.861	CHH&Co	Deming	9/10/1881	257.233	CHH&Co	W. Shoemaker
7/28/1880	256.183	CHH&Co	Deming	9/17/1881	225.343	CHH&Co	Soper
8/3/1880		CHH&Co	Ewing	10/3/1881	232.016	CHH&Co	Soper
8/3/1880	224.937	CHH & Co	Ewing	10/14/1881	207.053	CHH&Co	Colburn & Co.
8/7/1880	190.855	CHH&Co	Deming	10/19/1881	225.398	CHH&Co	Soper
8/11/1880	231.768	CHH&Co	Deming	10/27/1881	106.874	CHH&Co	W. Shoemaker
8/16/1880	241.584	CHH&Co	Deming	11/8/1881	111.862	CHH&Co	B F D
8/21/1880	240.554	CHH&Co	A C Gray Co.	11/15/1881	5.9	CHH&Co	S. C M
8/25/1880	222.91	CHH&Co	A R Gray Co	11/22/1881	136.922	CHH&Co	B F D
8/30/1880	229.012	CHH&Co	Deming	**1882**			
9/4/1880	210.771	CHH&Co	Deming	4/7/1882	121.595	CHH&Co	C J Co,.
9/9/1880	124.065	CHH&Co	Ewing	4/7/1882			
9/9/1880	103.274	CHH&Co	Ewing	4/10/1882	171.01	CHH&Co	E W Brooks
9/13/1880	207.145	CHH&Co	Perry	4/10/1882	73.588	CHH&Co	E W Brooks
9/16/1880	217.384	CHH&Co	Deming	4/15/1882	254.403	CHH&Co	Ac & K
9/20/1880	220.413	CHH&Co	Ewing	4/19/1882	60.061	CHH&Co	Ac & K
9/22/1880	256.197	CHH & Co	Deming	5/1/1882	250.815	CHH&Co	Chase & Pato
9/24/1880	225.836	CHH&Co	A R Gray Co	5/4/1882	258.275	CHH&Co	E W Brooks

LUMBER SHIPMENTS ON ALBRECHT/HUME

DATE	Board Feet 1000s	Where Cut	Consignee	DATE	Board Feet 1000s	Where Cut	Consignee
5/8/1882	35.462	CHH&Co	E W Brooks	8/4/1883	281.785	CHH&Co	B F Deming
5/8/1882	119.985	CHH&Co	E W Brooks	8/9/1883	269.878	CHH&Co	Streeh C & K
5/26/1882	250.69	CHH&Co	Houghton	8/13/1883	269.599	CHH&Co	A R Colburn
5/31/1882	266.5	CHH&Co	Chicago Lumber Co.	8/17/1883	154.904	CHH&Co	A R Colburn
5/31/1882	266.5	CHH&Co	Chicago Lumber Co.	8/22/1883	256.609	CHH&Co	A R Colburn
6/6/1882	22.531	CHH&Co	Chicago Line Co.	8/25/1883	180.075	CHH&Co	A R Colburn
6/6/1882	238.495	CHH&Co	Chicago Lumber Co.	8/29/1883	256.056	W Mann Co.	A R Colburn
6/10/1882	234.021	CHH&Co	Soper Bros	9/3/1883	259.012	CHH&Co	B F Deming
6/14/1882	226.55	CHH&Co	Soper Bros	9/8/1883	260.653	A V Mann	A. R. Colburn
6/19/1882	145.941	CHH&Co	Martin Wilson Co.	**1884**			
6/21/1882	209.816	CHH&Co	W. Shoemaker	4/16/1884	245.787	CHH&Co	A R Colborn
6/24/1882		CHH&Co	Soper Bros	4/19/1884	256.642	CHH&Co	A R Colborn
6/24/1882	200.161	CHH&Co	Soper Bros	4/26/1884	152.283	CHH&Co	no
6/30/1882	233.734	CHH&Co	Soper Pond	4/26/1884	18.334	CHH&Co	no
7/29/1882	225.068	CHH&Co	Soper Bros	5/2/1884	251.938	CHH&Co	Street C & Co
8/12/1882	280.617	CHH&Co	deming wood	5/7/1884	9.69	CHH&Co	A R Gray & Co.
8/21/1882	256.976	B & B	Kellly Rathbone	5/7/1884	288.846	CHH&Co	A R Gray Co
8/28/1882	225.146	CHH&Co	Soper & Pond	5/10/1884	81.12	CHH&Co	E W Brooks
9/2/1882	231.457	CHH&Co	Soper Bros	5/11/1884	191.681	CHH&Co	E W Brooks Co.
9/6/1882	224.87	CHH&Co	Soper Pond	5/14/1884	264.774	CHH&Co	A R Gray & Co.
9/11/1882	268.318	CHH&Co	Street & Co	5/17/1884	263.525	CHH&Co	B F Street C. Co.
9/14/1882	227.124	CHH&Co	Soper Bros	5/21/1884		CHH&Co	S K Martin
9/18/1882	257.268	CHH&Co	E B Simmons	5/24/1884	263.164	CHH&Co	B F D for C K G
9/22/1882	236.487	CHH&Co	Rawzin Root	6/6/1884	32.458	CHH&Co	B F D for S K M
9/26/1882	224.321	CHH&Co	Soper & Pond	6/16/1884	244.365	CHH&Co	BFD for S K M
9/30/1882	73.173	CHH&Co	Soper & Pond	7/7/1884	145.824	CHH&Co	Street C. Co.
9/30/1882	14.401	CHH&Co	Soper & Pond	7/17/1884	156.69	CHH&Co	B F Deming
9/30/1882	32.446	CHH&Co	Soper & Pond	7/23/1884	264.168	CHH&Co	Street & Kup
9/30/1882	10.92	CHH&Co	Soper & Pond	7/29/1884	278.438	CHH&Co	Street
10/10/1882	41.783	CHH&Co	Martin Wilson Co.	8/2/1884	231.349	CHH&Co	Street & Kup
10/10/1882	91.783	CHH&Co	Martin Wilson Co.	8/2/1884	35.454	CHH&Co	S C & Keep
10/10/1882	19.759	CHH&Co	Wilson Martin	8/13/1884	250.16	CHH&Co	Pond & Nelson
10/14/1882	220.872	CHH&Co	Soper Bros	8/14/1884	237.707	CHH&Co	Pond & Nelson
10/21/1882	237.9	CHH&Co	Soper & Pond	8/23/1884	271.076	CHH&Co	E W Brooks Co.
10/25/1882	219.588	CHH&Co	Soper Bros	9/15/1884	46.952	CHH&Co	BFD for C H & S
10/30/1882	236.409	CHH&Co	Soper & Pond	9/15/1884	15.51	CHH&Co	BFD for Curtis
11/6/1882	102.16	CHH&Co	Soper & Pond	9/20/1884	139.421	CHH&Co	BFD for E W B
11/6/1882	124.213	CHH&Co	Soper Bros	9/20/1884	117.431	CHH&Co	BFD
11/11/1882	101.313	CHH&Co	S K Martin	9/25/1884	106.87	CHH&Co	
1883				9/25/1884		CHH&Co	B F Deming
5/8/1883	270.602	CHH&Co	B F Deming	10/1/1884	259.691	CHH&Co	Silas Roseabille
5/28/1883	253.583	CHH&Co	E W Brooks	10/6/1884	107.863	CHH&Co	J Fransis Chicago
6/5/1883	248.138	CHH&Co	Kershaaw	10/6/1884		CHH&Co	B F D for H & C
6/8/1883	255.912	CHH&Co	B F Deming	10/11/1884	386.139	CHH&Co	B F Deming for EWB
6/12/1883	256.811	CHH&Co	T H Sheppard	10/17/1884	261.398	CHH&Co	Street C. Co.
6/15/1883	158.108	CHH&Co	B F Deming	10/29/1884	249.051	CHH&Co	W. Shoemaker Co.
6/15/1883	116.764	B & B	B F Deming	11/4/1884	87.129	CHH&Co	W. Shoemaker Co.
6/19/1883	111.199	CHH&Co	B F Deming	11/4/1884	171.753	CHH&Co	W Shoemaker & Co.
6/19/1883	157.763	B & B	B F Deming	11/8/1884	247.882	CHH&Co	BFD for A F Fisher
7/7/1883	181.682	CHH&Co	B F Deming	**1885**			
7/12/1883	231.106	CHH&Co	Gitchell Arm	5/2/1885		CHH&Co	B F D for H & Arp
7/16/1883	157.037	CHH&Co	B F Deming	5/2/1885	154.816	CHH&Co	BFD for H & Arp
7/20/1883	263.425	CHH&Co	B F Deming	5/8/1885	136.111	CHH&Co	H H Gardner & Co
7/27/1883	143.021	CHH&Co	B F Deming	5/8/1885	141.467	CHH&Co	H H Gardner & Co

LUMBER SHIPMENTS ON ALBRECHT/HUME

DATE	BOARD FEET 1000s	WHERE CUT	CONSIGNEE	DATE	BOARD FEET 1000s	WHERE CUT	CONSIGNEE
5/13/1885	265.154	CHH&Co	BFD for Fisher & W	7/29/1886	276.605	CHH&Co	BFD Rathborne
5/18/1885	304.583	CHH&Co	BFD Howell	8/3/1886	262.96	CHH&Co	S R Howell Co.
5/25/1885	133.241	CHH&Co	BFD for Fisher & W	8/7/1886	249.402	CHH&Co	Irsher & Witbeck
5/25/1885	148.087	CHH&Co	BFD Spring for Co.	8/11/1886	277.967	CHH&Co	Chicago Lm Co.
5/29/1885		CHH&Co	do for Shoemaker	8/17/1886	290.785	CHH&Co	Chicago Lm Co.
5/29/1885	209.799	CHH&Co	BFD for Shoemaker	8/21/1886	281.871	CHH&Co	Chicago Lm Co.
6/4/1885	289.029	CHH&Co	T W. Harvey	8/28/1886	280.805	CHH&Co	Chicago Lm Co.
6/9/1885	95.156	CHH&Co	BFD for H & Arp	9/2/1886	137.904	CHH&Co	BFD J Hotmeier
6/9/1885	197.948	CHH&Co	BFD for BFD	9/11/1886	275.488	CHH&Co	Chicago Lm Co.
6/13/1885		CHH&Co	do for Robinson & Co	9/17/1886	271.089	CHH&Co	Chicago Lm Co.
6/13/1885	142.587	CHH&Co	BFD for Robinson	9/23/1886	247.443	CHH&Co	BFD Louis Hutt
6/18/1885		CHH&Co	B F D /Robinson & P	9/28/1886	247.626	CHH&Co	BFD Louis Hutt
6/18/1885	236.595	CHH&Co	BFD for Robinson	10/25/1886	99.441	CHH&Co	BFD Holtmeier
6/23/1885	246.672	CHH&Co	BF Fisher & W	11/10/1886	242.297	CHH&Co	BFD E W Brooks
7/7/1885	247.322	CHH&Co	BRD for Vrsdmburgh	11/16/1886	264.955	CHH&Co	Chicago Lm Co.
7/14/1885	240.84	CHH&Co	Walter M Pond	11/22/1886	272.848	CHH&Co	Chicago Lm Co.
7/18/1885		CHH&Co	S R Howell	**1887**			
7/18/1885	201.254	CHH&Co	S R Howell	4/21/1887	279.128	CHH&Co	BFD Rathbom
7/24/1885	254.149	CHH&Co	BFD Fisher & W	4/25/1887	234.4	CHH&Co	C A Paltzer
7/28/1885	262.973	CHH&Co	C B Flnn	5/20/1887	101.368	CHH&Co	B F D Holtmeier
8/3/1885	255.156	CHH&Co	BFD for G H Parks	5/25/1887	262.684	CHH&Co	C A Paltzer
8/8/1885	285.347	CHH&Co	Soper Lumber	5/28/1887	258.702	CHH&Co	C A Paltzer
8/31/1885	268.827	CHH&Co	Soper Bros	6/8/1887	239.72	CHH & Co	S K W
9/5/1885	182.441	CHH&Co	Soper Bros	6/9/1887	254.86	BFD	BFD Street C
9/5/1885	90.72	CHH&Co	Soper Bros	6/11/1887	138.135	CHH & Co	S K W
9/12/1885		CHH&Co	BFD for HHG	6/13/1887	260.516	CHH&Co	O'Brien
9/12/1885	135.74	CHH&Co	BFD for HH Gardner	6/14/1887	237.548	CHH & Co	H B & Co
9/18/1885	224.661	CHH&Co	BFD for DFGChicago	6/16/1887	107.044	CHH&Co	BFD W J Nubes
9/23/1885	144.99	CHH&Co	BFD L. Hutt	6/23/1887	267.01	H G & Co	Shoemaker
9/23/1885	121.15	CHH&Co	BFD for L Hutt	6/27/1887	236.607	CHH & Co	S K W
9/29/1885		CHH&Co	do (Mkt)	7/1/1887	144.443	CHH & Co	S C & K
9/29/1885	179.363	CHH&Co	BFD (market)	7/7/1887	278.448	CHH&Co	C A Paltzer
10/6/1885	243.835	CHH&Co	BFD for S. Branch	711/1887	225.617	CHH&Co	A P & W E Kelley
10/10/1885	87.26	CHH&Co	do Holtmier	7/13/1887	230.272	CHH & Co	H B & Co
10/10/1885	35.874	CHH&Co	BFD Holtmier	7/16/1887	247.055	C & F	Shoemaker
10/17/1885		CHH&Co		7/25/1887	233.861	CHH & Co	S C & K
10/17/1885	227.733	CHH&Co	BFD Bmse Bader	7/30/1887	260.675	CHH&Co	C C Thompson & W
10/22/1885		CHH&Co	do for Holtmier	8/2/1887	237.241	CHH & Co	H B & Co
10/22/1885	125.774	CHH&Co	BFD J Holtmier	8/6/1887	82.763	C & F	W M
10/27/1885	261.064	CHH&Co	C B Hnn Co	8/13/1887	261.372	C & F	RR & Co
11/9/1885	230.665	CHH&Co	W Shoemaker	8/15/1887	265.124	CHH&Co	D F Groves
11/14/1885	264.641	CHH&Co	Adams Hasting	8/17/1887	58.807	C & F	do
11/19/1885		CHH&Co	do Babcock & Wheeler	8/30/1887	234.84	CHH & Co	S C & K
11/19/1885	116.297	CHH&Co	BFD Babcock & Wheeler	9/1/1887	259.521	BFD	BFD Louis Hutt
1886				9/14/1887	229.497	CHH & Co	S C & K
6/3/1886	291.6	CHH&Co	BFD Jos. Rachbourin	9/21/1887	257.344	CHH & Co	C B Fluer Co
6/8/1886	289.412	CHH&Co	BFD Jos Rachbourn	9/22/1887	253.77	CHH & Co	Shoemaker
6/12/1886	169.609	CHH&Co	A P & W E Kelly	9/27/1887	226.552	CHH & Co	S C & K
6/12/1886	118.841	CHH&Co	A P & W E Kelly	10/8/1887	255.064	CHH & Co	C J
6/17/1886	147.532	CHH&Co	BFD Market	10/14/1887	43.887	CHH & Co	do
6/21/1886	261.863	CHH&Co	BFD Market	10/28/1887	268.241	CHH&Co	Soper Lumber
7/20/1886	266.347	CHH&Co	C A Pattzer & Co.	11/2/1887	259.516	CHH & Co	BFD
7/24/1886	92.764	CHH&Co	A R Gray & Co.	11/2/1887	264.078	CHH & Co	Soper Lumber
7/24/1886	150.629	CHH&Co	A R Gray & Co.	11/7/1887	258.406	CHH & Co	Soper Lumber

LUMBER SHIPMENTS ON ALBRECHT/HUME

DATE	BOARD FEET 1000s	WHERE CUT	CONSIGNEE	DATE	BOARD FEET 1000s	WHERE CUT	CONSIGNEE
11/8/1887	147.333	CHH & Co	BFD	7/7/1890	289.465		A F Fisher & co
11/14/1887	261.988	CHH&Co	Soper Lumber	7/12/1890	297.505		A F Fisher & co
11/15/1887	253.057	CHH & Co	S K W	7/26/1890	285.113		A F Fisher & co
11/19/1887	258.158	CHH&Co	EW Brooks & Co.	7/30/1890	199.739		BFD A F Fisher
11/22/1887	74.598	CHH & Co	S C & K	8/5/1890	290.478		A F Fisher & co
1888				8/9/1890	276.883		BFD Chase & Pate
4/25/1888	270.031		Soper Lm Co.	8/23/1890	279.11		BFD Louis Hutt
6/4/1888	260.287		O'Brien Green & Co.	8/28/1890	286.314		BFD SB Barker & CO
6/8/1888	200.969		BFD D S Henry	9/11/1890	250.902		S R Fuller & Co.
6/25/1888	254.522		BFD Street Co.	9/16/1890	286.358		Watkins & Fuller
7/21/1888	240.483		BFD Ingtneyer	9/20/1890	234.307		Watkins & Fuller
9/3/1888	142.004		BFD L Hutt	10/9/1890	270.245		B F D Chase & Pate
9/8/1888	257.53		DB Banker & Co.	10/27/1890	82.648		BFD - J Holtmeier
9/12/1888	258.779		BFD Chase & Pate	11/3/1890	270.389		BFD Chase & Pate
9/17/1888	234.357		BFD Hutt	11/13/1890	150.672		BFD J Holtmeier
9/24/1888	242.989		BFD O'Brien Green	**1891**			
10/1/1888	141.481		BFD Holtmeier	4/15/1891	260.384		BFD Adam Schillo
10/5/1888	224.834		BFD C Schultz	4/20/1891	278.329		Watkins & Fuller
10/11/1888	137.244		BFD Holtmeier	4/24/1891	283.77		Watkins & Fuller
10/22/1888	251.905		BFD O'Brien Green	4/30/1891	278.661		Watkins & Fuller
10/27/1888	96.54		BFD Holtmeier	5/4/1891	265.702		BFD A Schills
11/2/1888	234.172		S B Barker & Co	5/9/1891	269.592		
11/7/1888	237.876		SB Barker	5/13/1891	292.053		
1889				5/19/1891	236.997		
5/15/1889	258.123		BFD Louis Hutt				
5/30/1889	221.514		BFD Louis Hutt				
6/4/1889	189.553		BFD Neebes				
6/17/1889	157.411		BFD O'Brien				
6/25/1889	267.836		BFD Chase & Pate				
7/6/1889	244.646		BFD Head & Sutherland				
7/11/1889	263.055		BFD O'Brien				
7/18/1889	276.734		BFD Adam Schills				
7/23/1889	191.925		BFD W Shoemaker				
7/27/1889	277.722		BFD Shoemaker				
8/1/1889	126.267		BFD Holtmeier				
8/20/1889	142.788		BFD Cook & Loomis				
8/20/1889	128.7682		BFD Cook & Loomis				
8/27/1889	258.051		BFD Blanchard				
8/31/1889	272.769		S. Martin				
9/4/1889	281.94		S K Martin				
9/13/1889	148.186		BFD Shoemaker				
9/27/1889	274.002		BFD Beidler				
10/2/1889	271.28		Edwin S Hartwell				
10/31/1889	257.62		BFD Chase & Pate				
11/6/1889	113.659		BFD Holtmeier				
11/6/1889	30.821		BFD Holtmeier				
1890							
5/26/1890	278.36		BFD A F Fisher				
5/30/1890	253.948		BFD Jos. Rathborne				
6/2/1890	279.517		A F Fisher & co				
6/6/1890	784.516		A F Fisher & co				
6/11/1890	300.892		A F Fisher & co				
6/28/1890	276.348		A F Fisher & co				
7/3/1890	264.757		AF Fisher				

INDEX

And
BIBLIOGRAPHY

Books

Andreas, A. T. *History of Chicago from the Earliest Period to the Present Time*, v. 2 (Chicago: A. T. Andreas Co, 1884).

Avery, Thomas, *The Mystery Ship from 19 Fathoms* (AuTrain, Michigan: Avery Color Studios, 1974).

Bold & Smithing's Manitowoc City Directory for 1880 (Manitowoc: Bold & Smithing, 1880).

Cooper, David, *Fire, Ice and Storm* (Wisconsin: State Historical Society of Wisconsin, 1991).

Chappelle, Howard I., *The History of American Sailing Ships* (New York: W. W. Norton & Co., Inc., 1935).

Falge, Louis, *History of Manitowoc County, Wisconsin*, v. 2 (Chicago: Goodspeed Historical Association, 1912).

Harms, Richard Henry, *Life after Lumbering: Charles Henry Hackley and the Emergence of Muskegon, Michigan* (Garland Publishing Co.: New York, 1989).

History of Muskegon County, Michigan, with Illustrations and Biographical Sketches of Some of Its Prominent Men and Pioneers (Chicago: H. R. Page & Co., 1882).

The History of Northern Wisconsin, v. II (Chicago: Western Historical Publishing Co., 1881).

Inches, H. C., *The Great Lakes Wooden Shipbuilding Era* (Vermilion, Ohio: H. C. Inches, 1962).

Jackson, Joe, *The Thief at the End of the World: Rubber, Power, and the Seeds of Empire*. (New York: Penguin Group, 2008).

Karamanski, Theodore J., *Schooner Passage: Sailing Ships and the Lake Michigan Frontier* (Detroit: Wayne State University Press, 2000).

Mansfield, J. B., *History of the Great Lakes*, v. 2 (Chicago: J. H. Beers & Co., 1899).

Marquis' Handbook of Chicago: A Complete History, Reference Book and Guide to the City (Chicago: A. N. Marquis & Co., 1887.

Marquis, Albert Nelson, ed., *The Book of Chicagoans: A Biographical Dictionary of Living Leading Men of the City of Chicago* (Chicago: A. N. Marquis Co., 1911.

Maybee, Rolland H., *Michigan's White Pine Era, 1840-1890* (Michigan History Division, Michigan Department of State: Lansing, 1973).

Pennington, Rochelle, *The Historic Christmas Tree Ship: A True Story of Faith, Hope and Love*. (Wisconsin: Pathways Press, 2008).

Plumb, Ralph G., *A History of Manitowoc County* (Manitowoc, Wisconsin: Brandt Printing and Binding Co.: 1904).

Ryckman, John W., ed., *Report of the International Maritime Exhibition, Boston, 1889*-1890 (Boston: Hockwell & Churchill, 1890).

Thompson, W. J., *Wooden Shipbuilding: A Comprehensive Manual for Wooden Shipbuilders to which is Added a Masting and Rigging Guide* (Chicago: A. C. McClurg & Co., 1918).

Twenty-Third Annual Report of the Commissioner of Labor, 1908: Workers' Insurance and Benefits Funds in the United States (Washington, D. C.: Government Printing Office, 1909).

Urquhardt, G. D. *Dues and Shipping in Foreign Ports: A Manual of Reference for the Use of Shipowners, Shipbrokers, and Ship Masters* (London: George Philip and Son, Ltd.: 1908).

Wenstadt, Tom, *The Freighters of Manitowoc: the Story of Great Lakes Freight Carrying Vessels Built in Manitowoc, Wisconsin* (Bloomington, Indiana: Authorhouse: 2007).

White, James T., ed., *The National Cyclopædia of American Biography*, v. 1 (New York: Jas. T. White & Co., 1898).

Wilson, James Grant, and John Fisk, eds., *Appletons's Cyclopædia of American Biography*, v. 2 (New York, D. Appleton & Co., 1888).

Journal Articles

"The Chicago River and Harbor," *Railway Age* (v. 31, no. 2: January 11, 1901).

Dopp, Mary, "Geographical Influences in the Development of Wisconsin. Chapter V. The Lumber Industry," *Bulletin of the American Geographical Society* (v. 45, no. 10) 1913.

Grant, Luke, "Industrial Democracy: The Longshoremen's Association," *The New Outlook* (v. 48, December 1, 1906).

Kohlmeyer, Fred W., "Lumber Distribution and Marketing in the United States," *Journal of Forest History* (April 1983).

John Halsey, "Shipwreck Preservation in Michigan: Two Decades On" *Contested Waters* Fall/Winter 1996, vol. 1(3/4)

The Jewelers' Circular and Horological Review, Volume 38, April 5, 1899.

Periodicals and Newspapers

Buffalo Enquirer
Chicago Daily Tribune
Der Nord-Westen (Manitowoc, Wisconsin)
Detroit Free Press
Herald Palladium
Manitowoc Pilot
Marine Record (Cleveland, Ohio)
Muskegon Chronicle
The Daily Interocean.
New York Times. October 30, 1878.

Unpublished Manuscripts

Gordon, Kellie Marie, "A Comparative Analysis Of The Deterioration Rates Of Textiles And Their Role In Determining Postmortem Interval ," unpublished thesis, The College of William and Mary, May 2003.

Francis, Maureen, "The Flush Toilet: A Tribute to Ingenuity," www.mastersplumbers.com.

Hansen, Stan B., "Book of Scales," unpublished, 2007.

Wilson, Loudon G., "Great Lakes Sailing Craft of the Past Years: A Collection of Data, Facts, and Diagrams Covering Commercial Sail Vessels on the Inland Seas during the Period from their Inception to their Demise," unpublished mss., Historical Collections of the Great Lakes, Bowling Green State University

Web Sites

http://www.perdurabo10.tripod, November 2010.

http://www.atrecovery.com/athome.htm, November 2010.

http://www.hal.state.mi.us/mhc/museum/explore/museums/hismus/special/schooner/questions.html, September 2010.

http://www.mygrannysatticantiques.com, October 2010.

http://www.thepotteries.org/allpotters/722.html, October 2010.

http://www.themuseumofceramics.org/pottery.html, October 2010.

Miscellaneous

Law of the United States Regarding Admeasuremnt of Vessels, Section 44 of the Act of August 4, 1790.

INDEX

I Am Still Here
by Lee Murdock

©2009 BMI

Oh, my name is Thomas Hume,
I was raised on the shores of Lake Michigan.
I served many a captain in my day.
From Muskegon port I sailed
out across the blue lake waters
to many distant harbors and fine bays.
But my sailing days are done,
like the setting of the sun
that I no more can see from where I lay.
And I can tell you now who visit me today,
that I'm still here, I am still here,
And my story you'll discover should you stay.

For over twenty years,
hauling lumber on the waves of Lake Michigan,
with my deck piled high
I'd throw the foaming spray.
Whether full dressed or reefed down,
stormy gale or in fine weather,
I carried cargo and crew without delay.
On a Thursday morn in May, in the year of ninety-one,
we set sail out from Chicago riding high.
The weather, it was fair, no prospects to deny.
Out of nowhere came, from out of nowhere came
A mighty squall, sent sails and sheets to fly.

Now many schooners sailed through the storms
and the squalls of Lake Michigan,
and some of those went missing o'er the years.
It was either from neglect,
bad luck or from poor seamanship,
their sad demise is chronicled in tears.
But on that fateful day when I settled in this clay,
after turning turtle in those rolling waves,
With my masts un-stepped and laid across my deck
displayed as by the hand of God.
By the hand of God
Lonely is my vigil as a ship betrayed.

So, my name is Thomas Hume,
I was raised on the shores of Lake Michigan.
I served many a captain in my day.
From Muskegon port I sailed
out across the blue lake waters
to many distant harbors and fine bays.
But my sailing days are done,
like the setting of the sun that
I no more can see from where I lay.
And I can tell you now who visit me today,
that I'm still here, I am still here,
And hope my story will outlive my hulk's decay.

Lee Murdock, singer, songwriter, and historian.

ABOUT

The
AUTHORS

Their second book together, Valerie van Heest and William Lafferty previously co-authored *Buckets and Belts: Evolution of the Great Lakes Self-Unloader*, winner of a 2009 Michigan State History Award from the Historical Society of Michigan. Together, they are partners in Lafferty van Heest and Associates, a museum exhibit design firm.

A member of the Women Divers Hall of Fame, **Valerie van Heest** has explored and documented shipwrecks for over twenty-five years, heading projects to document some of the Lakes' most important vessels, producing documentary films, designing museum exhibits, and writing for a variety of periodicals. In 2007, Valerie received the Historical Society of Michigan award for her distinguished volunteer service in the collection, preservation, and promotion of Michigan state and local history. Valerie is a regular presenter at museums, libraries, and film festivals, sharing the dramatic stories of ships gone missing on the Great Lakes, and has appeared on a variety of television news programs as well as the Discovery Channel. She is a founding board member of Michigan Shipwreck Research Associates and spearheads MSRA's search for ships lost off western Michigan, which has resulted in the discovery of several shipwrecks. She resides in Holland, Michigan, with her husband, Jack, and daughters, Cella and Taya. Her previous books included *ICEBOUND! the Adventures of Young George Sheldon and the SS Michigan, Buckets and Belts,* and *Lost on the Lady Elgin,* all winners of state history awards.

Twice winner of the Broadcast Education Association's History Award and winner of the Association for Great Lakes Maritime History's Barkhausen Award for original research in Great Lakes maritime history, **William Lafferty,** a former filmmaker, is an associate professor at Wright State University at Dayton, Ohio, where he has taught since 1981. He was born in Oak Park, Illinois, and grew up in the western suburbs of Chicago. As a child, he spent his summers in western Michigan, and continues to do so, where his interest in Lake Michigan's maritime history began. Over the years, he has developed an extensive collection of photographs and other materials pertaining to the history of shipping on the Great Lakes. A maritime historian, Bill's chapter entitled "Technological Innovation in Great Lakes Shipping: Leathem D. Smith and the Rise of the Self-Unloader" in "*A Fully Accredited Ocean: Essays on the Great Lakes,*" edited by Victoria Brehm and published by the University of Michigan, is a precursor to *Buckets and Belts.* Bill has a bachelor's and master's degree from Purdue University and a PhD from Northwestern University.

This book was made possible by the following organizations:

Michigan
Shipwreck
Research
Associates

Lakeshore
Museum
Center

MichiganHumanitiesCouncil

Michigan People, Michigan Places
Our stories, our lives.

Association for Great Lakes Maritime History

The Great Lakes Cruising Club

The Gertz Foundation